T0278185

BRIDGING THE SOFT SKILLS GAP

BRIDGING THE SOFT SKILLS

SECOND EDITION

SKILLS GAP

HOW TO TEACH THE MISSING BASICS TO THE NEW HYBRID WORKFORCE

BRUCE TULGAN

BESTSELLING AUTHOR OF
IT'S OKAY TO BE THE BOSS

WILEY

Published by John Wiley & Sons, Inc., Hoboken, New Jersey.
Published simultaneously in Canada.

For general information on our other products and services or for technical support, please contact our Customer Care Department within the United States at (800) 762-2974, outside the United States at (317) 572-3993 or fax (317) 572-4002.

Wiley also publishes its books in a variety of electronic formats. Some content that appears in print may not be available in electronic formats. For more information about Wiley products, visit our web site at www.wiley.com.

Library of Congress Cataloging-in-Publication Data

Names: Tulgan, Bruce, author.
Title: Bridging the soft skills gap : how to teach the missing basics to
  the new hybrid workforce / by Bruce Tulgan
Description: Hoboken, New Jersey : John Wiley & Sons, Inc., [2023] | First
  edition published in 2015.
Identifiers: LCCN 2022026726 (print) | LCCN 2022026727 (ebook) | ISBN
  9781119912064 (hardback) | ISBN 9781119912071 (adobe pdf) | ISBN
  9781119912088 (epub)
Subjects: LCSH: Soft skills. | Generation Y—Employment. | Business
  etiquette. | Personnel management.
Classification: LCC HF5381 .T757 2023 (print) | LCC HF5381 (ebook) | DDC
  658.3/124—dc23/eng/20220608
LC record available at https://lccn.loc.gov/2022026726
LC ebook record available at https://lccn.loc.gov/2022026727

Cover Image and Design: Wiley

SKY10035650_080522

This book is dedicated, yet again, to the great

—Susan Rabiner

Contents

PART ONE

THE SOFT SKILLS GAP

Prologue

Meet the Workforce of the Future

An executive in a major financial services institution recently told me about a recruiting interview with a very strong job candidate: "In the middle of my pitch about the long-term rewards of making a career in a company like ours, this young man starts laughing out loud. I mean actually laughing, just for a second. Then he quickly regained his composure. He was very apologetic. But what he said really struck me. He said, 'Sir, you must realize that it's very hard for someone in my position to have any kind of faith in those long-term promises. It's not that I don't trust YOU. It's just that I don't trust the future.'" The executive said, "What really struck me was that, of course, he's exactly right. There is so much complexity and uncertainty in the external risk factors. Why in the world would anyone trust the long-term promises of an institution like ours?"

The CEO of a biotech company in Silicon Valley was hosting a half-dozen employees at his weekly "lunch with the CEO." Making conversation with the 22-year-old brand new employee to his left, he asked, "Did you just graduate this past May or were you working somewhere else prior to joining us?" She said she had just graduated. The CEO said, "That's great. Congratulations. We are glad to have you." And then he asked, "Where did you go to school? What did you study?" The new young employee answered. The CEO continued, "Excellent. Did you do any part-time work while you were in school?" To this, the young woman replied, "Look, that's enough about me, all right? What about you? What's your story?" The CEO chuckled as he told me this story. He told me, "I wanted to say, 'My story? I'm your boss's boss's boss's boss. That's my story. But instead I just told her my story.'" He concluded, "It just took me aback, being so young and so junior in her role, her lack of inhibition in talking to the CEO of her new employer."

At the corporate headquarters of a very old and very large consumer products conglomerate, summer interns are sometimes permitted to attend certain high-level meetings, mostly as a learning experience, but also to run errands and assist with clerical tasks during the meetings. One such intern was visibly annoyed when she was asked by her manager to dress in "business casual attire, at least" on days when she would be attending such meetings. After "ignoring that suggestion entirely," the intern came to one such meeting "very casually dressed" and then spent most of the meeting texting on her handheld device. When her manager whispered quietly to ask her to please stop texting during the meeting, the intern responded in an exasperated tone, "Actually, no." The manager whispered back with incredulity: "'No'?" At this point, the intern explained, "I'm texting with my dad . . . about this meeting. So, it's fine. My dad works here!" As it turned out, she was giving a blow-by-blow account of the meeting in progress to her father, who was himself a longtime executive in the company, and had arranged the internship with the company for his daughter.

Some partners at a forensic accounting firm told me of their latest young associate "case study": This first-year associate, a recent top graduate of a top school, was cutting edge in his knowledge of a new set of tools and techniques for mining and analyzing data buried within evidentiary documents obtained during pre-litigation discovery. One of the partners said, "This kid had done some projects in school using this new approach and his technical knowledge in this area far surpassed anyone else in the firm. But he kept running into roadblocks because his communication made him seem so immature. At first, he couldn't get anybody to listen to him. Once we got him going on introducing the new process, I know it sounds petty, but he kept saying 'like, like, like' every other word and he could barely look people in the eye or string three words together without saying 'like.'" In short, "His inability speak in a way that seemed even remotely professional was just rubbing people the wrong way, especially in meetings, though it wasn't very much better when he was working with people individually." One of the other partners explained, "We had to send him to a class." One of the other partners added, "It took a lot more than one class."

A very savvy and experienced restaurant general manager shared this with me: "Schedule adherence is always an issue, but it's getting much worse. More and more we are having a terrible time with waiters, kitchen support, and cleaners disappearing for 'breaks' in the middle of their shifts, not to mention calling out 'sick' too often, coming in late, and leaving before shifts are over." To make matters worse, it seems that whenever confronted about their timeliness by a manager, often employees respond by pushing back. The general manager said, "They would always have an excuse and they'd be almost indignant about it. Every one of them is a 'special case.'" She reports: When his manager told him he was taking too many breaks, one waiter told his manager, "You have to understand, I have ADD so I am going to need some help staying focused." Reprimanded about coming in late and leaving early, a prep chef pushed back, "I'm not really used to following a set schedule." When confronted about regular last-minute absences, a cleaner explained, "Sometimes I just don't feel up to working."

In an aerospace company that hires hundreds of new engineers every year, engineering group managers have been reporting that lower-level engineers quickly become frustrated and bored with repetitive tasks and narrow recurring responsibilities – so bored in fact that they are playing games on their handheld devices while working. The problem, of course, is that the work of lower-level engineers – like so much work – involves a lot of repetitive tasks and narrow recurring responsibilities. One of the engineering group managers said, "If we don't actively keep them engaged in the work, they get distracted and then they slow down and they also start making more mistakes." Another group manager responded, "What are we supposed to do? I found it frustrating and boring when I had to do it too. The work is the work. Should we have the higher-level engineers do more of the grunt work so the lower-level engineers get a chance to do more interesting work so they will stay engaged? They are simply not as qualified yet to do the more interesting work."

An experienced nurse-manager on a busy hospital floor told me about her campaign to stop the nurses from using their handheld devices at the same time they are administering care to patients.

The manager and her nursing supervisors had been surprised and impressed to discover how often the nurses on their devices were instant messaging with each other about the patient care. They were asking each other for – and giving to each other – regular advice and support throughout the day. Sometimes they were searching the internet for clinical information – often reaching out on social media to other nurses who were not even coworkers. One supervisor was startled to discover a young nurse having a real-time video conference on her handheld device with her friend, a nurse in India. "She was standing outside this patient's room, discussing the case with her friend in India. When I asked her about it later, she said this friend had been a mentor to her in school and she felt like she didn't have anyone here yet she could confide in." By the way, the nurse manager hastened to add that the young nurse in question was NOT herself of Indian descent. She went on, "They spent a lot of time on FaceTime together. She was more comfortable getting answers from her friend in India than turning to any of us for help."

One large retail chain I know has a long-standing tradition of involving retail sales personnel in all aspects of the business – ranging from creative work, such as providing input on marketing, to janitorial work, such as cleaning the bathrooms in the store, and everything in between, including buying, inventory management, accounting, legal, HR, safety, loss prevention, and you name it. An executive in the company explained to me, "Of course, we have all those roles in the company: We have a professional marketing team, buyers, inventory managers, accountants, lawyers, and so on. We do use a janitorial service – they are not on their own cleaning the store. But we have a deep commitment to involving the store personnel in everything we do. We talk a lot about cross-training and teamwork. We do it because they are the face of the company to our customers and we want them to own everything in the organization." The executive added, "That's also one of the ways we recruit internally for corporate positions – not only store managers or district or regional, but also for other jobs throughout the organization." What's the problem? According to this executive, "They want to sit on the marketing panels, but they don't want to clean the store or change over inventory because those things happen after hours and seem less glamorous. They beg for the high-profile, fun, or interesting projects but they complain bitterly when they are asked to help clean the store or change over inventory. Quite a few of them outright refuse to do it. Quite a few have been fired or have quit over it." As a result, the executive concluded, "We are currently rethinking our whole approach to these cross-training/teamwork projects."

Senior leaders in US intelligence agencies have been grappling with the impact of steadily rising zero- to five-year employee turnover rates among new young intelligence professionals. This is a particularly pressing issue because intelligence agencies make an unusually large investment in new hires due to the elaborate selection criteria, the need to gain security clearance, the extensive requisite training, and the sensitive nature of the work and information to which employees are often privy. So, it is a big problem when that investment keeps walking out the door before the new young professionals have a chance to contribute to the mission. One intelligence official told me, "No matter how hard we try to develop a profile to help us select for retention – to predict who will be longer-term employees – it just doesn't work. We used to be able to do it. But it doesn't work anymore. Maybe there is no 'type' anymore who stays or a 'type' who goes. I'm afraid that the young people joining now who serve long-term will end up that way, not by deciding that today, but instead by deciding every few months or years to not leave just yet. We are making a lot of adjustments. But how are we supposed to identify the right high-potentials to start developing for new leadership roles? It makes succession planning very difficult. Too often those identified for promotion end up deciding to leave, taking with them the huge investment we've made in them."

Soft skills are more important than ever, in the new hybrid workplace, where we all must communicate, cooperate, and collaborate with an ever-widening range of people – whether remotely or in person. At the same time, there is a growing soft-skills gap throughout the workforce, and not just among the new young workforce, but also among people of all ages.

Managers tell us every day what one manager recently told me: "It's mainly about people skills. There have always been people who struggle with that stuff. But standards are dropping. I mean, even manners, but also work ethic, taking responsibility, and just working like you really care."

The incidence and insistence of managers reporting that soft skills are lacking in employees has risen steadily year after year since we began tracking it in the mid-1990s. There is a growing gap between the expectations of employers and the reality of how people manage themselves and their interactions with others.

Even when people show up with the latest and greatest tools and tricks, what they are missing – way too often and more and more – are the old-fashioned basics. What many refer to as "the soft skills."

Many business leaders and managers say something like, "This should NOT be our problem to solve! Shouldn't they have already learned all these old-fashioned basics from their parents? Or in kindergarten? Or at least in high school or college? Or graduate school for that matter? Or in work experiences? Or somewhere? Can't we expect employees to have the soft skills we need in order to get hired? The problem is that there is a perpetual shortage of good people with the technical skills so it's very hard to rule people out because you suspect they are lacking in soft skills."

Here's what I tell my clients: The soft-skills gap is your problem. That's the bad news.

Here's some good news: You can bridge the soft skills gap and doing so will give you a huge strategic advantage when it comes to hiring the best talent, getting them on board and up to speed faster, with better performance management, improved relationships, and greater control over retention.

We've collected hundreds of case studies of organizations and individual managers who have systematically helped their employees radically improve their soft skills. There are many, many ways you can help them build up one soft skill at a time, and make them better employees, coworkers, and future leaders.

Chapter 1

The Soft Skills Gap

*N*o matter how careful you try to be in your recruiting, selection, and hiring process, it is getting harder and harder to figure out which job candidates to hire. Should you hire the promising new graduate with impressive, freshly minted credentials indicating valuable technical skills, even though they seem like they might be yet another new potential hire lacking in some of those elusive yet critical "soft skills"?

It seems like a higher percentage of new hires are not working out, one way or another. What goes wrong? Too often they don't seem to appreciate that they are entering a pre-existing scene; joining an organization with its own mission, history, structure, rules, and culture; integrating with a group that has its own established dynamic; and engaging with individuals, each of whom has their own story and many of whom have been part of this scene in this organization for years on end or longer.

Too often they say the wrong things or speak at the wrong time – and they fail to ask the questions they should be asking. Heck, sometimes they can't even get to work on time. Anyway, they spend too much of the workday on their devices instead of focusing on the work. That really comes through in customer service scores, along with other complaints about front-line service personnel. Sometimes their lack of interpersonal skills leads to misunderstandings and even conflicts on the team.

You have to worry they have one foot out the door from the day they arrive, all the while asking for more of something – or more of everything. Even the superstars nowadays don't seem to want to come in early, stay late, work through meals and weekends and holidays, bend over backward, and jump through hoops like the superstars of yesteryear.

What is a soft skill? I use the term "soft skills" because most people understand the term is used, in contrast to "hard skills," which are technical, to encompass a wide range of nontechnical skills ranging from "self-awareness" to "people skills" to "problem solving" to "teamwork."

These skills may be less tangible and harder to define and measure than many of the "hard skills," but they are absolutely critical to the success or failure of any individual in the workplace. The problem is that these old-fashioned basics – professionalism, critical thinking, and followership – are out of fashion and so they are too rarely spoken of nowadays. Today's young talent is not being indoctrinated in these old-fashioned basics either at home or in school. Usually, by the time they get to the workplace, employers figure it is too late to focus on them. Certainly, most managers figure it is not their place, nor do they have the time or resources or know-how to deal with their employees' soft skills gaps.

So, the soft skills gap continues to grow, hiding in plain sight, despite the fact that it costs organizations a fortune every day.

I've asked tens of thousands of managers: "How much do these so-called 'soft skills' matter?" The answer is nearly universal: Soft skills matter a lot. The cliché is that people get hired because of their hard skills but get fired because of their soft skills.

When employees have significant gaps in their soft skills there are significant negative consequences: Potentially good hires are overlooked. Good hires go bad. Bad hires go worse. Misunderstandings abound. People get distracted. Productivity goes down. Mistakes are made. Customer service suffers. Workplace conflicts occur more frequently. Good people leave when they might have otherwise stayed longer.

It robs so many employees of greater success and causes so many managers so much aggravation and unnecessary costs. The soft skills gap is not a household term like the technical skills gap, but it should be because its impact is monumental.

Like the technical skills gap, the soft skills gap in the workforce has been developing slowly for decades. But the soft skills gap runs across the entire workforce – among workers with technical skills that are in great demand, every bit as much as workers without technical skills. What is more, the soft skills gap has gotten much worse in recent years.

How much of this can we blame on the newest youngest workers?

The Soft Skills Gap: Growing Steadily from Gen X to Millennials to Gen Z to Whoever Comes Next

Since 1993, I've been tracking the attitudes and behavior of managers and employees in the workplace and their impact on organizations, especially the impact on working relationships.

I started out as a frustrated young lawyer seeking to understand why the older, more experienced lawyers were so annoyed by those of my generation, Generation X (born 1965–1977). I quickly realized that it wasn't just the older, more experienced people at my firm who were annoyed with Gen Xers. It was nearly everybody older and more experienced in workplaces of all shapes and sizes.

That's when I started conducting in-depth interviews with young people and their managers, the original research that led to my first book, *Managing Generation X*. I formed a company to continue that research and we've been conducting that interview research for decades now, tracking workers of all ages, always including the ever-emerging and ever "newer" new young workforce. By the late 1990s, we were tracking the first wave of the great Millennial cohort (born 1978–1989). Then the second wave of Millennials (born 1990–1996), followed by Generation Z (born 1997 and later), and we'll interview new young workers as long as we endure.

Since the mid-1990s, I've had a front-row seat on the front lines and behind the scenes in organizations of all shapes and sizes. We've interviewed more than a half a million workers in just about every industry – health care, professional services, restaurants, retail, research, finance, aerospace, software, manufacturing, the public sector, even nonprofits, you name it. Based on two decades of research, I can report that the overwhelming data indicates a steady diminution in the soft skills of the workforce. Going forward, workers are increasingly likely to have significant notable weaknesses in one or several key soft skills.

Why is that?

Something Much Larger Is Going on Here: The Post-Boomer Generational Shift

Of course, the older, more experienced people are always more or less annoyed by the attitudes and behavior of each successive new young generation. New young employees are, by definition, always younger and less experienced and, therefore, lacking in the corresponding maturity and patience. As they step into the adult world with youthful energy and enthusiasm, young workers often clash with their older colleagues. That's always part of the story. But there is something much bigger going on here.

On a macro level, Generation Z represents a tipping point in the post-Boomer generational shift transforming the workforce. With Boomers retiring in droves, they are taking with them the last vestiges of the old-fashioned work ethic. The workforce of the near and intermediate future is a post-Boomer workforce – dominated in numbers, norms, and values by the Millennials and Generation Z as well as the aging Generation X. Plus, the workforce is even younger in Africa, South Asia, and South America.

The new workforce is fundamentally shaped by this era of profound change and uncertainty driven by a confluence of epic historical forces:

GLOBALIZATION

We are all global now, whether we like it or not – connecting and traveling to work across borders in every direction and combination. We can all look forward to a future of interdependency and competition with a rising global workforce from every corner of this ever-flattening world.

TECHNOLOGY

The pace of technological advance today is unprecedented. Information. Computing. Communication. Transportation. Commerce. Entertainment. Food. Medicine. War. In every aspect of life, anything can become obsolete any time – possibilities appear and disappear swiftly, radically and often without warning.

INSTITUTIONAL INSECURITY

In the post-9/11 era, we all live in a world threatened by terrorism and environmental cataclysm, a world where the economy fluctuates wildly from boom to bust, governments sometimes shut down or run out of money, and great companies conquer or fail or merge or continually downsize, restructure, and reengineer. Our greatest institutions are in a perpetual state of flux in this constantly changing world.

It's harder and harder for people to anchor themselves reliably to even our greatest institutions.

THE INFORMATION ENVIRONMENT

Gen Zers are the first true digital natives, but we've all been learning how to think, learn, and communicate in a never-ending ocean of information facilitated by handheld supercomputers. We all live in an information environment defined by internet ubiquity, wholesale technology integration, infinite content, and immediacy. From a dangerously young age, we have infinite access to information and ideas and perspectives – unlimited words, images, and sounds – a context completely without precedent.

HUMAN DIVERSITY

In every dimension, the world is becoming more diverse and more integrated. Generation Z will be the most diverse workforce in history, by far. That's true in terms of geographical point of origin, ethnic heritage, ability/disability, age, language, lifestyle preference, sexual orientation, color, size, and every other way of categorizing people. Equally important, Millennials and Gen Zers tend to look at every single individual, with their own combination of background, traits, and characteristics, as their own unique diversity story. They value difference, uniqueness, and customization, most of all their own. Meanwhile, the entire workforce will include a global mix like never before.

At the same time, the emerging workforce is increasingly shaped by two very important microtrends:

HELICOPTER PARENTING ON STEROIDS

By the late 1990s, the Boomer-esque self-esteem-based "everyone gets a trophy" style of parenting was morphing anew. "Helicopter" (hovering) parenting has been appended with the even more aggressive "snowplow" (clearing away obstacles) strategy. As one Gen Xer parent told me, "I don't want to make my kid just feel like a winner no matter what happens. I want to do everything I can to set him up with every possible advantage to make sure he has a big head start in the real world so he can win for real." Parents (and contingent authority figures) are thoroughly engaged in supervising and supporting the child's every move, validating their differences, excusing (or medicating) their weaknesses, and setting them up with every material advantage possible.

Young people today spend so much of their time ensconced in their own highly customized safety zones – the private comfort of protection and resources provided by responsible adults who are always supposed to be looking out for them. They expect authority figures to be always in their corner, to set them up for success, and to be of service. They are often startled when authority figures see it otherwise.

VIRTUAL REALITY

It's not just that they are always looking down at their handheld devices. Today we are all always plugged into an endless stream of content and in continuous dialogue – through social media–based chatting and sharing and gaming – with peers (and practical strangers), however far away (or near) they might be. We are forever mixing and matching and manipulating from an infinite array of sources to create and then project back out into the world our own ever-changing personal montage of information, knowledge, meaning, and selfhood.

We can try on personas, virtually. Social media makes it easy to experiment with extreme versions of one persona, or another; more or less (or much more) a crass means of expression.

The youngest among us are perfectly accustomed to feeling worldly and ambitious and successful by engaging virtually in an incredibly malleable reality – where the stakes can seem all-important one moment, until the game is lost and reset with the push of a button.

Soft Skills Are – Sort of – About Conforming in an Age of Nonconformism

If you think about it, soft-skills are mostly about "fitting in" –making an effort to conform one's attitude and behavior to established standards of conduct – in order to engage and work together effectively with others in a shared enterprise.

Here's the thing: The workforce of the future will be the ultimate nonconformists in an age of nonconformism.

For some time now, the pendulum of the zeitgeist has been swinging – more or less – away from conformism. Nonconformism is the belief that it is better for individuals to be unique and emphasize their individual differences from the group; conformism is the belief that it is better for individuals to subordinate their individual differences and adopt the normative/dominant attitudes and behaviors accepted by the group in order to "fit in." Of course, in any era, there are conformists and outliers, regardless of the zeitgeist. But the pendulum does swing one way or the other: Think of the relative conformism of the 1950s – when so many were trying to assimilate and come together after the global upheaval of World War II and its aftermath. The revolutionary nonconformity of the 1960s yanked the pendulum in the other direction and it's been swinging that way ever since. There have been ebbs in the swing – notably in the middle 1980s and the years immediately following 9/11. Still, the pendulum has kept swinging away from conformism and toward a broad cultural relativism – for many good reasons.

It is unfortunate that cultural relativism has been widely misunderstood and is often misappropriated – in a classic case of reductio ad absurdum – by those who wish to argue that no expectations of conformity to any norms of conduct are legitimate. This is the kind of thinking that leads to the wishful notion that "all styles are equally valid."

The problem with that notion should be obvious. If everybody has their own style and some styles are mutually exclusive, then how are we all supposed to get along and work together in a shared enterprise? Try to imagine a communication system where everybody speaks their own language. Or picture a style of greeting strangers by punching them in the nose. These suggestions are ridiculous.

Yet, there are, in fact, many different ways to greet a stranger appropriately, depending upon the community – or the time period – in which you live: Some people would bow. Others would shake hands. Some would hug. Others kiss on both cheeks. More and more people are bumping fists these days, partly due to the rise in awareness of especially pernicious contagious germs. Social norms are indeed highly variable depending upon context – manners and etiquette, appropriate attire, hairstyles, good grammar, even the very meaning of words in the same language. When I was working in Ireland in the 1980s, I asked a woman for a "ride" home. It turns out I should have asked for a "lift": "ride" meant something very different in Ireland from its most common meaning in the United States. Perhaps nowadays asking someone for a "ride" in Ireland would be less shocking, with so much more shared global media. To wit, social norms also change over time.

It is easy to see why cultural relativism is so important to understand. It provides much of the intellectual underpinning behind some very important long-term cultural/social trends away from oppressively hierarchical systems and one-size-fits-all rules. Strict hierarchy and one-size-fits-all rules are extremely limiting: By design, they prescribe and proscribe the behavior of those who wish to belong. They constrain individual expression, creativity, and innovation. They exclude those outside the norm or unwilling to conform. Sometimes they exclude people for very bad reasons, sometimes even with malice, as in, "No Irish Need Apply," a sign common in US workplaces in the mid- to late nineteenth century. Cultural relativism teaches us that differences in norms and values are not an indication of moral failure. There may be many different ways to think about or do things that are equally legitimate, on some fundamental level, even if they might be more or less appropriate in one culture versus another. Plus, being open to people with differing norms and values can lead to valuable new opportunities and possibilities. Still, none of this means that "all styles are equally valid."

What it really means is that a style that may be appropriate in one time and place may not be appropriate in another. As any cultural anthropologist will tell you, the way to get along in a different culture is to adjust your attitude and behavior to what is appropriate in that place and time. That doesn't mean you have to compromise your values or integrity or abandon your "true self." It just means that if you want to develop good relationships with others and be effective, you need to be adaptable.

Dress codes offer a simple example. I often say, "If you don't want to wear a uniform, you shouldn't become a police officer, a firefighter, or a soldier." Uniforms function to help police, firefighters, and soldiers to identify each other in a crowd; signal to outsiders the special role of those in uniform; provide important information such as name and rank; and have built-in equipment for doing the job. Uniforms can make a lot of sense in some jobs. So where do you draw the line? What about suits and ties for men? Skirts and jackets for women? When I was a young associate at a Wall Street law firm in early 1990s, there was a serious brouhaha among the young associates over women lawyers being required to wear skirts instead of pants. In the 1990s! The Gen X lawyers had a mini-revolt in favor of women being able to wear pantsuits. What rebels! This may seem like a bit of ancient history, yet "skirts versus pants" for women was truly contested ground in many workplaces well into the 1990s. The inequity of the requirement for women was hiding in plain sight.

Some standards of conduct are more burdensome than others. Some are arbitrary, exclusionary, constraining, and worth resisting. Others are necessary, efficacious, and worth some inconvenience. How does one tell the difference? This question holds the key to bridging the soft skills gap with today's young talent.

The bottom line is this: You simply cannot have a functional workplace where everybody makes their own rules of conduct. Imagine an organization where some employees support the mission, but others support the opposite mission. Where nobody agrees about who is in charge. Where people come and go whenever they feel like it. Where some people wear pantsuits and others wear bathing suits. Where people only work on the tasks and responsibilities they enjoy, insist on doing everything their own way, and only work with the people they like. Where meetings are held with no particular agenda and people are encouraged to blurt out whatever pops into their heads. Where people may or may not return each other's calls and emails. And so on.

Sometimes conforming makes a lot of sense. Consider the essential soft skills such as the elements of professionalism, critical thinking, and followership. These are old-fashioned basics for a reason: They are time-tested best practices. They work.

Nobody needs workers of any age, shape, size, or persuasion to give up their uniqueness as individuals, their overall nonconformism, or adopt too many arbitrary, exclusionary, or overly constraining standards. But most managers would very much like their employees to make some reasonable adaptations – to adjust at least some of their attitudes and behaviors to the realities of the adult workplace.

The Soft Skills Gap: The Missing Basics in Today's Workforce

The problem is that more and more of today's workforce are neither accustomed nor inclined to conform their attitudes and behavior for an institution or an authority figure.

They apply for the job. They accept the job. They might be excited about the job. They might want your approval. They usually are very keen to succeed. They definitely want the paycheck. Nonetheless, they usually do not realize just how much "just doing their own thing" makes their attitudes and behavior maladaptive in the real world of the workplace.

Many have no concept of the incredible power of the old-fashioned basics. They are usually just not familiar with the old-fashioned basics – and certainly, they have very little experience. And like any skill, if one does not practice, one simply cannot master the essential soft skills.

Let's go back to the ur-conundrum of the soft skills gap: The promising new candidate with impressive credentials – especially in-demand technical skills – who is nonetheless lacking in soft skills. If you interviewed them privately, as I do all the time in my research, they would probably say something like this: "I have, like, the hard skills they need. So they, like, shouldn't care so much about the soft skills? So I come in a little late or leave a little early or blow off the occasional day? So what?! They should just, like, tell me what they need me to do? Give me, like, the resources I need. And I'll get the job done. Why do they keep, like, insisting I do everything their way? Their way, like, makes no sense! My way is, like, so much easier. And I'm, like, not afraid to say so!"

This person is in a real quandary. It is a quandary shared by so many workers – not to mention their coworkers and managers – everywhere I go. Today's workforce has so much to offer – technical skills, ideas, perspective, energy. Yet too many of them are held back because of their weakness in a whole bunch of old-fashioned basics.

What are the soft skills that so many people are missing nowadays that managers miss the most? There are so many of them. I've boiled them down to some key behaviors in three old-fashioned categories:

1. Professionalism;
2. Critical thinking; and
3. Teamwork.

Let's take a closer look.

#1 OLD-FASHIONED "PROFESSIONALISM"

Why don't people today hold themselves to a higher standard when it comes to their attitude, work habits, and people skills?

There are five reasons:

First, the newest workers are usually coming to you straight from school. So, maybe they have the most in-demand technical skills, coming from college or university, or maybe graduate school. That means they've probably become quite accustomed to a very luxurious situation: Room and board are not only covered, but also arranged conveniently in close proximity to campus. College students are surrounded by their peers all the time and often with intimate friends. College students have access to the resources of a major institution, but their only responsibilities are those of a valued customer. They have the support and services of staff, administration, and faculty, but their social status is determined by where they fit in with their peer group. Their "job" is a privilege for which someone else is paying (even if it is paid for by student loans, the tremendous cost of all this is deferred). They have very little supervision and a great deal of latitude in all manner of their personal habits and conduct. How many college students who come to work for you have gotten in the habit of staying up too late hanging out with their friends? Skipping too many classes? Doing their work at the last minute . . . or not at all? Then expecting to receive an inflated grade?

That takes me to the second reason: More and more of the new workforce has been raised by helicopter parents on steroids. Even after they arrive in the workplace, young workers are only a phone call (or text) away from their parents. Maybe they are on their own now, for the first time, after being reared by parents (and their parenting posses) who did a lot of the work for them of closely scheduling, managing, and supporting their every move. With their parents doing so much of the work, many young workers never mastered the basics of taking care of themselves.

Third, the customization of everything – growing for decades now – has entrenched in the newer workforce a fundamental expectation that individual accommodation is the norm. Even if they, themselves, did not homeschool, never had an ILP (an Individual Learning Plan, very common in schools nowadays), and never took meds for their special "diagnosis," they surely grew up among kids who did. And surely too many people told them each and all, way too often, "You are a special case." Meanwhile, there has long been a growing current of personal customization in every sphere where consumers dwell – especially media. Of course, all of this dovetails with the long-term zeitgeist swing toward relativism – i.e. "all styles are equally valid." Increasingly, the basic assumption is that workers should be able to just "be themselves" and "express" their true identity at work.

Fourth, when it comes to people skills, it is easy to blame the fact that people of all ages have become so accustomed to electronic communication that they are losing the ability to communicate well in-person. That's surely a big part of the story. Communication practices are habits and most people are in the habit of remote, informal, staccato, and relatively low-stakes interpersonal communication because of their constant use of handheld devices and the mores of social media and instant messaging.

Fifth, much of what older, more experienced people might see as matters of professionalism – attitude, self-presentation, schedule, and interpersonal communication – today's workers are more likely to consider highly personal matters of individual style or preference and really none of their employer's business.

#2 OLD-FASHIONED "CRITICAL THINKING"

Why are today's workers not better at "thinking on their feet" – learning, problem solving, and decision making in their own heads without a device?

What managers tell us regularly in our interviews is summed up well by one senior-level nurse manager with more than three decades of experience managing nurses:

> They just don't think on their feet the way they used to. They know a lot. But if they are not sure of something, they go right to their device. If there is not an obvious online resource to answer their question immediately, then they turn right to another person – whoever is available – another nurse, a doctor, or anyone they run into next. What they never seem to do [enough] is just stop and think. They can often find the "right" answer, but often they don't always fully understand the answer they've found. It's not just a lack of experience. It's a different way of thinking. They don't puzzle through the problem and they don't stop and reflect on why the right solution is the right solution.

Why don't they stop and think on their feet, puzzle through problems, and reflect more on the best solutions?

Of course, there is one big reason: So many people today have never had the need. Today's information environment offers infinite answers to every question under the sun and they've always had powerful, easy-to-use information technology at their fingertips all the time.

On this subject, I often remind older, more experienced people, "Do you remember when we used to have conversations with very smart people about meaningful things that sometimes ended with a giant chorus of 'I don't know,' 'I don't know,' 'I don't know,' and 'Neither do I'? Or maybe you remember having those 'I wonder if ____' conversations with yourself." Are you old enough to remember those conversations? Well, young people today have never had that conversation – with themselves or anyone else. As long as they can remember, when they reach that point in a conversation – "I wonder if ____" – they (or someone else) would go immediately to a handheld device to get answers, or a short related video, or a giant detour that distracts them from the original inquiry altogether.

With computers and content providers to do so much of their thinking for them, so many people nowadays have hardly any experience digging deep, puzzling, and reflecting. They have a built-in expectation that learning curves are instant. They think of learning in small increments – filling skill and knowledge gaps as they run across them. The long learning curve is a rarity and a bit of a mystery.

When it comes to the learning habits of most of today's workforce, most experts blame changes in the emphasis of the education system at all levels. Teaching to the test has been way too common for far too long. It is all too rare that schools teach students to assemble and evaluate evidence, construct multiple competing arguments and understand multiple sides in a debate, untangle seeming inconsistencies, and wrestle with complexity. In college, university, and graduate school, those learning technical skills are likely to continue throughout their education on that "learning for the test" pedagogical trajectory. Those being schooled in the liberal arts often err all the way on the other end of the spectrum. Young liberal arts graduates may become so convinced that "all styles are equally valid" that they have difficulty vetting information for legitimacy, use-value, and broader implications in the real world.

This takes me to another disturbing factor in today's information environment: the proliferation of half-baked experts spewing content on just about everything. Nowadays you can find an expert to support nearly any proposition: "My expert says that two plus two equals five." What is one supposed to do with information like that? Yet such information is everywhere. The impact of this factor goes way beyond the common internet search misfire in which "two plus two equals five." Far more damaging, the organic pluralism of the internet has led to a false sense of intellectual pluralism, a world in which people think, "Maybe two plus two does equal five." This has led to profound distortions in the public discourse – in all media – in which pure fiction, gut feelings, and opinions are given the same weight as well-researched facts, rigorous analysis, and strongly constructed arguments. This phenomenon dovetails with the swing of the zeitgeist pendulum toward cultural relativism more generally and with the weakening of institutional credibility. After all, what authority figure in what institution has the staying power to say, definitively, that "two plus two must equal four"?

Maybe we shouldn't be so shocked when they sometimes tell us, "It appears that two plus two may actually equal five." After all, in virtual reality, this equation probably has very few negative consequences. It's only now that they are entering the real world of the workplace where – all of a sudden – their lack of skill and experience in the basics of critical thinking can have very real consequences.

#3 OLD-FASHIONED "TEAMWORK"

Why don't people today respect authority – in terms of citizenship, service, and playing your role?

"Question Authority!" has not been a slogan for a long time, but is a rather hackneyed cliché. So maybe it is too easy to explain away today's workforce's seeming disregard for joining something larger and making personal sacrifices for the greater good.

Why don't more people value citizenship, service, and playing one's role on the team?

Four reasons:

First, people today think more like customers than like players. Yes, they know that their employer is the one paying them. But still, they look at their relationship with any established institution, no matter how small or how large, and they think, "What do you have for me? And what currency do I need to use to get what I want/need from you?"

Most workers are grateful to have a source of income and maybe some benefits. They are grateful to be accepted, validated, and wanted. They are grateful to have access to a hub of resources from which to acquire experience, training, networking – a place to be, with computers and phones and bathrooms, maybe a kitchen or a gym, and possibly some office supplies. They are grateful for the future doors that might be opened by this current job. But let's not get carried away. It's not as if they are likely to be here for a long time anyway.

Most people today realize they are much less likely than those of prior generations to have long-term uninterrupted careers with one organization. They are also unlikely to be exclusively employed by one organization at any given time, to work full-time and on-site, or to trust the "system" or the organization to take care of them. Thus, they tend not to show what looks like loyalty – a desire to belong, deference to authority, a willingness to make short-term sacrifices for the good of the whole, and an eagerness to contribute regardless of credit or rewards.

Second is the way workers today think about their relationships with coworkers not in positions of authority. These relationships involve a high degree of interdependency in pursuit of concrete goals every step of the way, and the stakes are high. Adults are in the workplace to earn their livelihoods. There are lots of opportunities to disappoint and/or be disappointed.

Third is how they look at individuals in positions of authority. Once again, they think like customers. In this case, specifically, your customer! Workers do not typically look at other people in the work-place trying to figure out "their proper place" in the context – how to adapt in order to "fit in" with others who clearly have long-standing relationships and a well-established course of dealing (i.e. an estab-lished way of doing business together). Instead, they look at you – and everyone else in the room – and think, "I wonder what role you might play in this chapter of my life story?"

Fourth, almost nobody anymore is planning to follow the old-fashioned career path, so they figure they are probably just passing through your organization anyway. Why go to a whole lot of trouble adapting to your approach to how they should manage themselves when they won't even be here that long? They are thinking, "Seriously, what am I supposed to do? Adapt my schedule and work habits and style and attitude for every new job?" Even if they could be convinced to adapt for an employer eventually, they are very unlikely to be ready to do it from the get-go, certainly not early in their first or second real job.

Face the Hard Realities of the Soft Skills Gap

Maybe you are thinking, "Wait a minute. I know plenty of people who are great at professionalism, critical thinking, and teamwork!" Of course, you do! And I do too! It seems like now is a good time for me to make it clear that even nowadays, there are many people with excellent soft skills. It's just that there are not enough of them – it's a matter of supply and demand. That's especially true among people with in-demand technical skills, of whom there is a shortage to begin with. Over and over again, we hear from leaders and managers at all levels that the soft skills gap is not going away. If anything, it is getting worse. And it's not just about the youngest people in the workplace. Overall, this gap has been developing for decades. The costs are great, the opportunity costs are even greater, and yet the problem stands right there in plain sight, not even hiding. Why does this problem evade solutions?

There are three reasons:

First, you cannot hire your way around the soft skills gap, at least not entirely. If you are hiring for a low-supply, high-demand technical skills job, you probably won't be able to select out all those with weak soft skills. If you are hiring for nontechnical jobs, then soft skills are among the only criteria, making the demand for those with strong soft skills very high, despite the low supply.

Second, soft skills cannot be spoon-fed to people or forced upon them. Soft skills are all about the regulation of the self. They must be fully embraced in order to be learned. You have to get workers to care enough about soft skills that their self-building drive is activated and focused on mastering the missing soft skills.

Third, you probably don't have a bunch of extra time or resources to pull your people out of work and send them for soft skills training, or to create your own boot camp (like the Marines) to break down every worker and systematically rebuild them. If you are like most managers, then you deal with soft skill gap issues when they arise – when an employee is late, or inappropriate, or makes an error in judgment, or when there are conflicts on the team or a bad customer service interaction. You deal with the problem. Maybe you note the issue. Maybe if it is a recurring, ongoing issue with an employee, you really drill down and try to deal with the problem. In any case, unless you are the rare exception, your approach to dealing with the soft-skills gap is pretty much ad hoc, hit or miss.

In our training seminars, when I start talking about these difficult realities, managers start nodding their heads and listening carefully. I often say, "I don't have any easy answers because easy answers work only in fantasyland. What I do have is a lot of difficult partial solutions." That's when managers in the real world know that I really have something to offer them. All I do in my seminars is teach managers how to imitate the best practices that the most effective managers are doing successfully every single day. How are the most effective managers bridging the soft skills gap in their organizations, as a daily routine?

Here's the number one thing they have in common: They recognize the incredible power of soft skills – in themselves and others, and in organizations and teams. They understand what can go wrong when individuals, teams, or organizations have big gaps in their soft skills. Even more important, they understand how much can go so incredibly right – the extraordinary potential for added value – as a result of unlocking the power of soft skills. Consequently, they build soft skills development into every aspect of their people strategy and management.

Chapter 2

You Can't Hire Your Way Around the Soft Skills Gap

You can shine a bright light on soft skills in every aspect of your human capital management practices:

- Staffing strategy and hiring
- Onboarding and up-to-speed training
- Performance management and talent development
- Ongoing training
- Management and leadership

But you simply cannot hire your way around the soft skills gap.

There are many sectors of the labor market where significant education and credentials are not required threshold criteria for employment – these include many service or quasi-service jobs in retail, restaurant, cleaning, warehousing, moving, mining, agriculture, and so on. The available talent pool in this sector offers many diamonds in the rough, but few are fully refined when it comes to soft skills. Yes, you can (and should) poach the most polite cashier, waiter, janitor, etc., from your competition across the street, but that strategy only goes so far. Even your best hires in this sector will require significant onboarding and training to get up to speed – not just in the basic tasks of the job, but also in your high-priority soft skills.

At the next tier of the skill spectrum is the sector of the labor market in which substantial technical training may be required, but may be done in less than a year. Sometimes this training is provided by a public or private vocational education program, often affiliated with local employers. In other cases, employers provide pre-employment training or extensive on-the-job training. These jobs range from construction and assembly and mechanical repair work to bookkeeping to food preparation and sales. These programs are intended to provide job-ready employees. What always amazes me about the training for these roles is how they focus almost exclusively on the hard skills and pay only lip service to soft skills training. Then they complain bitterly about the soft skills of these employees, especially the youngest among them.

At the highest end of the labor market, the very threshold criteria for employment include years of education and formal training. If you are hiring engineers, doctors, nurses, medical technicians, accountants, actuaries, financial advisers, law enforcement officers, teachers, data analysts, code makers, code breakers, enterprise level management, and so many other roles for which the supply is far below demand, then you are squarely in the middle of the technical skills gap that gets so much of the attention in the media. It takes so much time, energy, and money – so much personal investment on the part of the individual employee – to acquire these in-demand skills that employers are in fierce competition for them. Employers often have so few candidates with the requisite hard skills that they simply cannot rule people out because of seeming gaps in their soft skills. Of course, no matter how highly trained they may be in the hard skills, new employees still require onboarding and up-to-speed training in the systems, policies, and practices of their new employer. Again, I am always amazed at how little attention is given to soft skills training in the onboarding and up-to-speed training process.

The bad news punch line in this quick lesson on contemporary labor market dynamics is that you cannot hire your way around the soft skills gap and, therefore, you simply must plan to address it in every aspect of your human capital management. The good news corollary is that you can hire smarter and give yourself a competitive advantage by making some slight adjustments in your staffing strategy, recruiting, and selection of employees.

Staffing Strategy and Hiring

Yes, you need to hire people who have or can learn the required technical skills. Yes, if you are hiring at the high end, you have no choice but to hire those who have acquired the necessary education and training. Yes, there is a limited supply. No, that doesn't mean you can ignore soft skills in your hiring.

Nowadays, all the attention in the talent wars is going to the technical skills gap. Yet, every day in our work, the stories managers tell us about good hires gone bad and bad hires gone worse are about failures in the soft skills, not the hard skills. That's true in every sector. It is rare that managers tell us a new hire failed because of a lack of technical skills. Nine times out ten, an unsuccessful hire fails due to soft skills, not hard.

Never forget, one very good hire is much better than three, four, or five mediocre hires. No matter where you are on the skill spectrum, build in soft skills criteria systematically in every aspect of your staffing strategy and hiring process:

STEP ONE

For every single position, build a profile and job description that includes not just the key hard skills for that role, but also the key soft skills. Use our competency model to start your brainstorming, but make them your own. Once you identify the high-priority soft skills behaviors for each position, name them yourself. Describe them in detail. Build those criteria into the basic job requirements in no uncertain terms from the very outset. Be prepared to turn away candidates who do not meet these soft skills criteria just as you would turn away candidates without the necessary hard skills. Or else, if you are forced to hire people without the required soft skills, make sure you have a plan in place to address those soft skill gaps from the first day of employment, just as you would have a plan in place if you hired an employee without the necessary technical skills.

STEP TWO

Look for talent from sources well known for the strong soft skills you need. If you are hiring out of schools and training programs, definitely find out which ones include soft skills in their standard curriculum. If you are poaching talent from other employers, poach from employers known for their strong soft skills training. This is why so many employers want to hire those who have served in the military: You can be sure that most people who have served successfully in the military will display respect for authority, willingness to wear a uniform, excellent manners, timeliness, consistency, follow-through, teamwork, and initiative. The same goes for anybody who makes it to Eagle Scout. Maybe it is the Peace Corps, or an NGO, a club or church or an athletic team; maybe you are looking for someone who has run a marathon, worked as a camp counselor or schoolteacher, or volunteered in a soup kitchen. What schools, employers, or organizations do you know where members or alumni are likely to have stronger soft skills in the areas that matter the most to you? Create a shorthand list of clearinghouse talent sources, successful participation in which is an indicator that job candidates are likely to have stronger soft skills. Then pay special attention to candidates with those soft skills "credentials" on top of their hard skills credentials. But don't wait for them to come to you. Be proactive about seeking candidates from those sources. If you can build relationships with key influencers in those sources – teachers, career counselors, leaders, active members of organizations, military outplacement personnel, and so on – they can help you identify good candidates, which will also earn them a positive reputation for helping good people find good jobs.

STEP THREE

Include your high-priority soft skills behaviors in your employer branding and recruitment campaign messaging. That's why it's so important to name your high-priority soft skills – to help you create meaningful slogans to capture them. Of course, there is always the iconic "the few, the proud, the Marines" as an example. That message is a signal to applicants that this job is going to be very demanding of them on a very deep level. Your recruitment message says a lot about how you see yourself as an employer. If you advertise for automobile mechanics by saying, "hiring qualified automobile mechanics," you are not really saying much. If your message is "looking for super smart automobile mechanics who can solve problems and are great team players," that says a lot more. Remember, the goal of any recruiting campaign is to deliver a compelling message in order to draw a sufficiently large applicant pool so that you can be very selective. Your goal is to draw mechanics who – at least – aspire to be very smart, good problem solvers, and great team players. You want to draw applicants who are looking for a job where they can learn and grow and build themselves up. We call it a "self-building" job. You want to draw applicants for whom the idea of self-building is a big turn-on, not a turnoff.

STEP FOUR

Start with a bias against hiring. Look for red flags. The biggest mistake hiring managers make – especially when hiring for low-supply, high-demand technical skills – is continuing the "attraction campaign" until the job candidate has accepted the job and sometimes until the new employee is already at work. We call this "selling candidates all the way in the door." In a tight labor market, the pressure to hire leads to hard selling a job to a candidate, even if that person is not ideal for the job. In fact, so many employers are so starved for talent that they just can't bear to turn potential employees away, even in the face of huge red flags. If someone comes late for the interview or falls asleep during the interview or has typos in their résumé – and timeliness, good health, or attention to detail are important soft skills for this job – then those red flags are telling you, "DON'T HIRE THIS PERSON!"

STEP FIVE

Build a selection process that places a heavy emphasis on high-priority soft skills. Here's a shortcut: Scare away job candidates who only think they are serious by shining a bright light on all the downsides of the job. If you need to hire nurses with especially high levels of grit and patience, make sure to tell them early in the selection process that they will sometimes be expected to help orderlies change bed pans. If you need to hire engineers with especially high levels of diligence, make sure to tell them right away there will be plenty of late nights and weekends coming very soon. Whatever the worst, most difficult aspects of the job may be, start your selection process with vivid descriptions of those downsides. Then see which candidates are still interested in the job. They are the ones worth testing and interviewing.

We recommend using research-validated testing wherever possible to get a quick baseline reading of an applicant's aptitude in key areas of the job, including high-priority soft skills. Whatever test you settle on, just make sure you can implement and evaluate it with relative speed. And make sure you know in advance exactly what you are looking for. What are you testing for? If you need an employee who can write well, simply hand the applicant a piece of paper and ask them to write something. If you need an employee who can speak well, ask them to prepare a brief presentation and then present it. If you need an employee who can solve problems in spatial relations, give them a puzzle. If you need an employee who can solve math problems, give them some math problems to solve. If you need an employee who can be on time, schedule three interviews, at three different times. And so on. Of course, some soft skills are harder to test for than others.

Then comes the job interview, the one employment selection process almost every manager does, but very few do well. When it comes to interviewing, the best practice is still the simple model of behavioral interviewing. Although there are entire courses taught in the topic, I often teach it to managers in my seminars in three minutes. Behavioral interviewing simply means asking applicants to tell you a story and then listening carefully to their story. When you are doing behavioral interviewing, make sure to ask applicants not only about their use of hard skills, but also their use of soft skills: "Tell me a story about a time you solved a problem at work." Or, "Tell me a story about a conflict you had with another employee at work. How did you solve it?"

Finally, consider one last stage of selection, which we call "the realistic job preview." This might be a probationary hiring period, or an internship before the real job, during which you can try out the employee and the employee can try out the job for a while. Make sure to assign them real tasks that mirror the actual tasks, responsibilities, and projects they will be asked to do if they accept the job. Make sure to include the grunt work. Another option is a period of "job shadowing" or "tagging along" with another person in your organization who is doing the same job this person will be doing if hired. This approach is sometimes used in hospitals. Make sure the would-be health care workers get to see sick patients, bedpans being emptied, and some of the other tough tasks they'll have to handle. By tagging along for several days, a week, or more, your applicant will get a good picture of what the job entails. You will also get the double bonus of having the existing employee who is shadowed spend a lot of time with the applicant in the job setting. This often leads to existing employees coming in and saying, "Hey, I hope we are going to hire this person!" Or, "Hey, we are not going to hire this person, are we?" Their feedback will tell you a lot. If applicants can't shadow, perhaps you can give them an opportunity to watch people doing the actual job – either in person or on live or recorded video. Sometimes on factory floors or in restaurant kitchens, the best thing you can do is let a prospective employee watch people actually doing the work for a little while and make sure they know what they are getting themselves into.

STEP SIX

If there is any lag time between the time an offer is made and accepted and day one of the actual job, take advantage of that time. Maybe the employee needs to finish school, or the employer must complete a security screening. Use the delay to keep sending the message about your high-priority soft skill behaviors. Send the new hire books, videos, or other targeted learning materials. In every way you can, keep sending the message that those soft skill behaviors really matter.

Onboarding and Up-to-Speed Training

Ask yourself: What happens when your new employees walk through the door on day one? How do you leverage those first days and weeks?

You won't be surprised that my platinum standard for onboarding and up-to-speed training is the Marine Corps Boot Camp. For 13 solid weeks, they provide an all-encompassing 24/7 experience in which they take an ordinary human being and transform that person into a marine – a person with a unique set of self-management skills, critical thinking skills, and people skills – a person so connected to the Marine Corps and its mission and every other marine that this person is now ready to walk into the line of fire, literally, and win battles.

You don't need obstacle courses and firing ranges. You don't need to make your newly hired employees do push-ups in the sand in the middle of the night. But take the lesson: What message are you sending about standards and expectations for high-priority behaviors from day one?

First, make sure you know exactly what happens with your new hires in the formal orientation, onboarding, and up-to-speed training. Most employers have only a minimal process for welcoming new employees and getting them on board and up-to-speed. Obviously some employers are better at this than others. Typically employers provide a basic introduction to the mission and history of the organization (or not); after this, employees get the basic facts and figures (or not), meet some of the key players (or not), receive a primer in the policies and paperwork (or not), and maybe some of the rules and traditions (or not).

Second, consider the inevitable handoff to the hiring manager (maybe that is you), once the official orientation program is complete. That's where so much of the real onboarding action is going to happen and that's exactly where the ball is so often dropped. Don't drop that ball.

If you want to send the message that those behaviors are truly a high priority, then you have to pay more than lip service. How much of your onboarding and up-to-speed training is dedicated to spelling out performance standards and expectations for those high-priority soft skill behaviors? How much time is dedicated to championing those behaviors and teaching them?

Here's a pretty simple rule: It should be about half.

As one savvy leader in a very successful retail chain put it to me: "For every hour we spend teaching a cashier how to operate the register, we spend at least an hour teaching them customer service skills – how to interact with customers and how to solve their problems."

Of course, it doesn't have to be half and half. Maybe the best approach is to have a dynamic integrated approach to onboarding and up-to-speed training that is designed in every way to send a powerful message about high standards and expectations for employees' attitudes and behavior in relation to work.

One of my favorite companies is a rental car company that prides itself on hiring only college graduates for every position, no matter how entry level. They also pride themselves on an onboarding process that not only teaches every new hire the business, but also makes it 1000% clear to new hires exactly what kind of workplace citizenship is expected of every single employee. On top of hours upon hours of training, with computer-based tools, and hands-on coaches, new hires can expect to find themselves out in the parking lot washing cars. Everybody in this organization – from the top to the bottom – is expected to wash cars. Nobody is too important to wash cars. In between washing cars, new hires are expected to study. And study they do, because each week they must demonstrate proficiency in a range of subjects including the company's computer system, details about the company's fleet, insurance, reservations, sales, marketing, customer service, billing, administration, problem solving with everyday situations, corporate philosophy, and on and on. The training materials spell out everything new hires must learn from week to week. And they study every night because – from day one – they are expected to be working, helping out in any way they can, during the day. There are also weekly coaching sessions with a fellow employee – each new hire is assigned a coach. There will be tests – at the 30-day mark, at 60 days, and at 90 days. This incredibly impressive program, which the company runs on-the-job in thousands of rental car shops all over the world, not only teaches new hires how to run the business, but also inculcates a powerful sense of the kind of work ethic and commitment the company requires. The results can be seen in every corner of this world-class organization. Their onboarding program is not exactly the Marine Corps Boot Camp, but it is truly profound in its impact.

Of course, onboarding and up-to-speed training needn't be profound. Let me give you a more mundane example. In one large company that hires a lot of new engineers, managers and more experienced engineers were increasingly frustrated with some of the work habits of many of their new engineers, including their email communication habits. A senior director of engineering in this company told me: "When it came to email, they did a bunch of things that drove everybody crazy: They would do every email "no-no": red flag emails indiscriminately, cc too many people on emails, or reply all to the wrong things, fail to change subject lines. But in particular they would send lots of very short email messages from their handheld devices instead of composing a proper email. We developed a list of dos and don'ts for email communication and we built in a 30-minute module in orientation." How did that work? "Problem solved."

I have a very similar story from a top accounting firm: Managers in this firm had noticed a growing pattern of "poor meeting manners" among new staff accountants. What are "poor meeting manners"? According to one senior partner: "Poor attendance, late arrival, constantly looking at their devices, lack of preparation, interrupting, going way off topic, making inappropriate comments . . . I could go on." The solution was very similar: The firm began explicitly teaching new hires how to prepare for and conduct themselves in meetings. It was so successful, the firm leadership decided to overhaul everybody's "meeting manners." As it turned out, it wasn't just the new associates whose meeting manners were not so great. After they developed the meeting manners program, the leadership realized that everybody in the firm could benefit from learning and observing these best practices for meetings. As a result, said the senior partner, "We had a real change in our culture around meetings. People in this firm became religious about following the rules of conduct. Our meetings got much better and they remain so. It's a centerpiece of our culture now."

Gee, maybe that's mundane and profound at the same time.

Performance Management and Talent Development

Most large organizations have some sort of formalized performance management system, and nowadays more and more are extending those systems to also take a more structured approach to talent development. The essence of performance management and talent development is simple. It's all about continuous improvement:

- ◆ Setting clear goals
- ◆ Monitoring and measuring actual performance in relation to those goals
- ◆ Providing feedback, direction, and guidance
- ◆ Problem solving and troubleshooting
- ◆ Identifying opportunities to speed up or increase quality
- ◆ Recognizing and rewarding success
- ◆ Identifying high performers for key assignments, opportunities, and promotions

Organizations with formalized systems typically start with annual or quarterly corporate goals and then cascade those larger goals down the chain of command, to each division, department, team, and individual. This is to create alignment from the top to the bottom – so everybody is moving in the same direction at the same time. In any case, at the individual level, employees typically spell out goals for themselves – annual goals and quarterly goals, and if they are smart, they then take the process further to monthly, weekly, and maybe even daily goals. Usually these goals are primarily focused on key performance indicators – revenue or profitability, maybe, or else productivity (output) or quality (negative error rate) – related to the individual employee's specific tasks, responsibilities, and projects. While soft skill behaviors have a huge impact on any individual's performance when it comes to key performance indicators, the specific behaviors may not be spelled out explicitly or identified as specific goals in a performance management system.

Usually, when soft skill behaviors are spelled out – if at all – in a formal performance management system, it would be in one of two cases:

- If an employee is failing to meet performance goals, then corrective measures might be spelled out in terms of an employee's specifically related suboptimal soft skills behaviors. The problem is that by this point it's often already too late. If you wait until an employee has demonstrated a track record of failure on a key soft skill behavior, then the performance management system is probably going to serve simply as a way to document that failure and provide a paper trail to help fire that person.
- Soft skill behaviors might be included as part of an individual's personal goals and/or for "professional development." The problem is that this is often the part of the employee's performance goals that are given the least weight and the least attention. Employees are likely to give these goals weight and attention in direct proportion to how much the organization does.

As a seasoned leader in a top financial services firm told me:

> Your people can tell if you really take this stuff seriously and they
> can tell if you don't. If you measure it, they pay attention. If there
> are consequences for failure, they pay attention. If there are rewards
> for success, they pay attention. When you identify top performers,
> the smart ones look and see, "What makes that person successful?"
> If that person is rewarded and promoted despite their failures on
> those soft skills, people pay attention to that. They say, "Oh, if you
> make your numbers, that's what really matters." But if you hold
> people back when they fail on those soft skills, despite making the
> numbers, then people pay attention to that too. What you measure
> and what has consequences and what gets rewarded, that's what
> your people are going to focus on.

Your employees can only focus on so many things at once. And
you can only focus on so many things at once. If high-priority behaviors are truly high priorities, then you need to make that clear with
real stakes in your performance management, and talent development. Whether you have a formalized system or not, remember,
whatever you measure and what has consequences and what gets
rewarded, that is what they are going to focus on.

If you want your employees to really focus on high-priority soft
skill behaviors, then you need to manage them very well, through
high-structure, high-substance teaching style management.

Your employees need to know exactly what is expected and
required of them when it comes to high-priority soft skills behaviors – every step of the way. They also need to know that their performance will be measured and that the score will have real
consequences for failure and real rewards for success.

Ongoing Training

Now I should say, "I have good news and bad news." If you succeed
in getting your employees focused on building up their performance
on high-priority soft skills, then the next question they are going to
ask is, "Exactly what training resources can you provide me for
improving in these areas?" That is both the good news and
the bad news.

Why is it bad news?

One health care executive captured the explanation in simple terms:

> We invest so much in education and training for our new professionals, that we have gotten a reputation among our competitors as a great place from which to poach talent. We invest in them through internal programs and also tuition reimbursement for everything from a one-day seminar to pursuing an advanced degree. It is a great tool for recruiting and morale. But it also paints a target on our back. The other hospitals in the region actively recruit our two-year employees. Of course, they are thinking, "You've been working there for two years? Perfect. Come work for us and we'll get the return on their education and training investment." It's very frustrating!

We call this the "development investment paradox." You invest in developing your new talent only to make them more valuable in the free market, where they are in danger of selling your development investment to the highest bidder. This is problematic when it comes to hard skills training as well as soft skills training: But it is especially maddening with soft skills training because soft skills are broad, transferable skills that never become obsolete and will make your employees more valuable anywhere they go in any job. Plus, if you think of soft skills training as "extra" rather than "mission critical" then it seems like a foolish investment to make altogether.

What are the answers to this paradox?

1. Use this paradox as an important reminder of the wisdom of sourcing new talent by targeting employers with great reputations for building up the soft skills of their new employees.

2. Be prepared: If you become one of those employers known for building up the soft skills of your new employees, you are going to become a target for talent poaching. Think of your competitors sitting around a table: "Their front-line employees are so great – they seem so solid, well put-together, smart, capable, polite, engaged, and engaging!

What can we do to lure them away?" That's a problem you DO want to have. However, it puts a high premium on retaining the great talent you are going to be developing.

3. Calibrate your development investment every step of the way so you never go too far out on a limb. But don't fool yourself: High-priority soft skills behaviors ARE absolutely mission-critical. That's why it's so important to know precisely which behaviors are your high priorities and focus on them like a laser beam.

4. You need to get your employees to really buy into the value of the high-priority behaviors so they truly own the learning process and are prepared to share the costs of the investment. That means you need to engage their formidable self-building drive. If their self-building is engaged, they will spend lots of time on self-directed learning outside of work and, when they are at work, will be purposely focused on demonstrating and practicing their growing repertoires on the job.

5. Provide them with as many easy-to-use targeted learning resources as you possibly can to support their self-directed learning. These can be low-tech resources just as much as high tech, but remember they are going to be very tuned in to just-in-time learning resources available online. In particular, today's talent is used to being able to get a simple tutorial on just about any topic by going straight to a short online videos with explanatory articles (or multiple videos from multiple sources). If you want to have some input on the sources from which they learn, that means building and supporting easy-to-access learning resources that are in alignment with your training goals.

Does this all mean that you shouldn't be so generous when it comes to less targeted investments in soft skills? You have to do the math for yourself, but I will say this: Whatever investments you make, the key to protecting your investment is making your employees full partners – co-investors – in the learning process. As long as they are actively learning skills they value – with your support – they are much less likely to think about leaving.

The general manager of a restaurant from a well-known chain recently shared this with me:

> When we teach our team members customer service skills, obviously it's all about taking care of our customers. But a huge part of our emphasis is on the value to our employees as well. Sometimes they don't realize at first that customer service skills are extremely valuable in any role in any organization. So we hammer away at the fact that every minute they spend learning and practicing customer service skills is not just an investment in this job but also an investment in they are making in themselves. We need them to buy-in so we really sell it to them.

"How does it work?" I asked. He continued:

> It really works because we really help the team members own it: Every day there is a quick team huddle and in every meeting a different team member takes a turn leading a quick customer service lesson. They can take a lesson from our curriculum or they are free to create their own lesson. They find cool videos and articles and quotes and some of them really get into it. We take this very seriously – so we recognize and reward team members when they go above and beyond, financially and otherwise. We often add the lessons they create to our curriculum and we give them full credit as content creators. It creates a virtuous cycle: Some of them really get into it and they make a point of actively practicing the techniques on the job and really showing off what they are learning. Of course, they are usually the ones who stay and become assistant managers and start moving up through the company.

Lessons learned:

◆ If you want your employees to buy in, then you have to really sell it to them: Take the time to make the case for why the skills you want them to learn are not just good for you and your business, but are also going to be really valuable to them. Remember, soft skills are broad, highly transferable skills that are valuable in any kind of job and never become obsolete.

◆ Help them own the learning by giving them a concrete role in the process: How can you get them actively involved in the training? Can they bring some of their own ideas to the table? Can they help you define learning goals? Identify sources of content or create original content? Teach some of the lessons?

◆ Make sure they have opportunities to practice what they are learning on the job and gain recognition, reward, and advancement through active participation. Pay close attention to the employees who really get into it as they are likely the ones who might stay and build careers in your organization.

Remember that today's workers are highly accustomed to self-directed learning: If they are eager to learn something, you cannot hold them back in today's information environment. They will go out into the endless sea of information and people online and navigate their own course of links and sources. Before you know it, they will be surprising you with their thoughtfulness, originality, and engagement in the learning.

Whether you are hiring people to wait tables in a restaurant, dig ditches, or engage in high-level sales, if you can get them to own the learning process, they are going to be thinking more and more about how they do whatever it is they do. Remember, knowledge work is not about what you do but how you do whatever it is you do. If you help them make whatever they are doing knowledge work by constantly trying to leverage soft skills in their work, they are going to become more and more invested in that work, more and more engaged, and better and better at their jobs.

One very smart manager in a large pharmaceutical company observed:

> As soon as they join my team, I have new team members develop their own individualized learning plan for targeted technical and non-technical learning. They need to learn our product line with all the technical specifications. But it's every bit as important that they learn how to show up very professional in their look and demeanor. They need to know how to get a doctor's attention and hold the doctor's attention. I want my reps to seem intelligent and sophisticated, not just knowledgeable about our products.

The pharma manager continued:

The funny thing is that, with the technical stuff, I can drill that into their heads. But with the soft skills, that's more like getting in shape. I can't go running and do push-ups for you. You need to go to the gym if you are going to get in shape. So the individualized learning plans are really great when it comes to the soft skills: I have them map out their learning goals in detail. For every goal, I have them go out and do research and create a list of learning resources. Those resources can be books, videos, people in real life or in their online social networks, article links, web sites, or really anything else. That process alone, of doing that research, has quite an impact. They learn so much just going out and researching the learning resources. Then I have them make a learning plan with concrete learning goals and specific lessons related to the goals. They keep a learning log of the lessons they've done, the work product involved if any, the learning goals they've accomplished, and how the learning is making a real impact on their actual work. This also becomes a regular part of our team meetings – sharing learning resources and sharing lessons.

"What is the best part about this approach?" I asked. The manager replied:

The best thing about this is that they do so much of the work of their own training. Plus they are mining the internet for learning the resources and usually the bulk of the resources they find are basically free. On top of that, they end up doing such a good job harnessing those resources, organizing them and sharing them, that they are actually building up a great training curriculum at practically no cost to the company. Some of the stuff they come up with is so good and so well targeted to what we need because they are motivated to find the right material to help them on the job. And they do most of it on their own time.

The Human Element: What Role Are You Going to Play?

Whether you are in a large, complex organization with lots of resources or a tiny business where you are the chief cook and bottle washer, the most important element in bridging the soft skills gap is the human element.

If you are not an active champion of high-priority soft skills behaviors in your sphere of influence and authority, then you can be sure that the talent in your midst will not buy in. If key leaders are not walking the talk – and talking the walk – they will simply roll their eyes at the best slogans and logos. No matter how vividly clear the messaging and training has been throughout the hiring and onboarding process – even if key soft skill behaviors are part of their individual performance plans – if their leaders do not emulate the high-priority behaviors themselves and emphasize them in their day-to-day management, workers will not believe the organization is serious. As much as they may seem to take their cues from peers or online sources, you can be sure that they will take their cues about what aspects of performance really matter from the authority figures with whom they interact most.

Sure, you need to get your employees to own their soft skills learning process and make available lots of easy-to-use online resources so they can pursue their own self-directed learning. But that doesn't let you off the hook. You've got to spend time with them – in person whenever possible – to lead them to purposeful self-directed learning, and you need to spend time with them during the intervals between their learning sessions.

The very nature of soft skills is such that they are very hard to develop without the help of another human being who can serve as an objective third-party observer and source of candid feedback. Ideally, that human being would be one who is a bit older and more experienced, perhaps one with greater influence and authority – and one who can provide guidance, direction, and support.

What role are you – and other leaders in your organization – going to play in bridging the soft skills gap?

If you are leading, managing, or supervising any person on any project for any period of time, you have an obligation to provide regular guidance, direction, support, and coaching to that person on every aspect of that person's performance – including their perfor-mance on high-priority soft skills behaviors. The problem is that it's so easy –in the day-to-day grind of work – to put these issues on the back burner. Most managers don't spend much time talking with their employees about their soft skills development, unless they are dealing with a specific instance of failure. Right? When do managers most often talk with their direct reports about matters of self-management or critical thinking or people skills? When an employee is late or dressed inappropriately or loses something or fails to follow through or makes a "stupid" mistake or curses at the wrong time or has a conflict with a customer or a coworker . . . or something else that is a petty failure.

That's why managers often say things like, "Do I really have to talk to my employees about these things? They are adults. They should already know how to manage themselves and solve problems and play well with others." Sorry. You really have no choice. If you are in charge of anybody, then it is part of your job.

At the very least, you must build it in to your regular management routine. Talk about the high-priority soft skills in team meetings and talk about them in your ongoing one-on-one dialogue with every single person you manage. Focus on the high-priority behaviors in your organization, your team, and each role, or those that are particular focal points for particular individuals. Trumpet the broad performance standards regularly. Just like every other aspect of performance, build it into your team communications and talk about it on a regular basis in your one-on-one dialogues. Require it. Measure it. Reward people when they do it. Hold people to account when they don't.

Become a Teaching Style Manager

Managers often ask me, "At what point can I back off on giving them so much attention?" My answer: "Whenever you want to start losing that employee's best efforts."

Surely some employees need more attention than others. But they all need your attention. The superstars want to be recognized and rewarded, but they also want managers who are in a position to help them do more, better and faster, and earn more for their hard work. Low performers are the only ones who don't want their managers' attention, but they need it more than anyone. And mediocre performers – the vast majority of employees who are somewhere in the middle of the performance spectrum – often don't know what they want from a manager. But the fastest way to turn a mediocre performer into a low performer is to leave that person alone without any guidance, direction, support, or coaching. Your job is to lift up all those employees and help them do more work, and do it faster and better every step of the way. Not just because that's good for business, but also because continuous improvement is the key to keeping people focused and motivated.

The best employees today want managers who know who they are, know what they are doing, and are in a position to help. They want managers who spend enough time with them to teach them the tricks and the shortcuts, warn them of pitfalls, and help them solve problems. They want managers who are strong enough to support them through bad days and counsel them through difficult judgment calls. They want to know you are keeping track of their successes and helping them get better and better every day. That's what I call a "teaching style manager."

Being a "teaching style manager" means:

- ◆ Talk about what's going right, wrong, and average every step of the way.
- ◆ Remind everybody of broad performance standards regularly.
- ◆ Turn best practices into standard operating procedures and teach them to everybody.
- ◆ Use plans and step-by-step checklists whenever possible.
- ◆ Focus on concrete actions within the control of the individual employee
- ◆ Monitor, measure, and document individual performance in writing.
- ◆ Follow up, follow up, follow up, and provide regular candid feedback.
- ◆ Ask really good questions.
- ◆ Listen carefully.
- ◆ Answer questions.
- ◆ Get input.
- ◆ Learn from what your employees are learning on the front line.
- ◆ Think through potential obstacles and pitfalls – make backup planning part of every work plan.
- ◆ Anticipate and prepare.

- Train and practice.
- Strategize together.
- Provide advice, support, motivation, and even inspiration once in a while.

Teaching-style management is also how you can help your most ambitious people who are so eager to take on more and more challenges and responsibilities. People so often tell us, "I can do so much more than I am doing. I want to do so much more than I am doing. But I don't want to do more of the same. I want to do something new and different." While this desire is a valuable impulse on the part of self-starting high performers, it also poses two significant challenges to their immediate managers:

1. Their job is to get the work done, whatever the work happens to be. Sometimes there are no new and interesting challenges. But wait. That doesn't need to be the end of the discussion. Help them make their current work new and interesting by teaching them to leverage knowledge, skill, and wisdom to do their work better, whatever that work happens to be. As soon as they walk in the door, have every new employee create an individualized learning plan in which they map out their responsibilities, and for each responsibility, make a list of learning resources (books, people, specific websites). Encourage them to set learning goals and then keep a journal of what they are learning and how they are using it on the job.

2. If you have truly new and interesting challenges for your employees, then you will have to make the time to teach them how to do that new and interesting work. You can't just give them a new challenge and say, "Figure it out." The secret is to teach and transfer just one small task or responsibility at a time. Make sure the person masters each new task or responsibility before you transfer another. You can train them the old-fashioned way in short-term stages that track directly with adjustments in their day-to-day responsibilities. Every new task turns into a proving ground, which enables them to demonstrate proficiency and earn more responsibility right away.

Don't fall for the myth that people today only want to learn from computers. That's nonsense. They want to learn from people. They want to learn from you.

Take It to the Next Level

If you want to take it the next level, go beyond regular performance coaching. Make teaching and learning the soft skills basics an explicit part of your mission and goals for your team going forward.

I know this seems like way too much to take on for some managers. Maybe you are thinking: "I am not a teacher or trainer. And I certainly don't have the time – nor do my employees – to get bogged down in soft skills training." Beware of this thinking. If you are reading this book, you are probably struggling with the soft skills gap in your organization or on your team.

The second half of this book is dedicated to helping you teach the missing basics – complete with step-by-step lesson plans. Imagine the impact you could have if you dedicated just one or two hours per week to building up the soft skills of your team. In just those one or two hours, you can make them aware, make them care, and help them learn the missing basics one by one – one step at a time. You can build them up and make them so much better.

Chapter 3

Unlocking the Power of Soft Skills

So many business leaders and managers at all levels fall for the myth that soft skills are a "nice to have" rather than a "must have" – simply a luxury they cannot afford to prioritize. That is a huge mistake.

Hard skills are easier to define and measure, yes. Hard skills are critical and they deserve lots of attention, but don't let anybody fool you: Soft skills are every bit as important. For the vast majority of your workforce, soft skills are the key to your success in the workplace and competitive differentiation in the marketplace. Soft skills are the source of a huge amount of power that is always right there hiding in plain sight – a tremendous reservoir of often untapped value – a secret weapon for any smart organization, team, leader, or individual performer.

Yes, the hard skills – the technical skills – are absolutely required in any job. That's every bit as true at the low end of the skill spectrum as it is at the high end. Right? Even if you are a cashier in a convenience store, you simply must know how to operate the cash register and make change to do the job. That's the bare minimum. After all, you can't do the job if you can't do the job. But that's only half the story.

The many soft skills which I put into those three old-fashioned buckets – professionalism, critical thinking, and followership – are where even the most technically proficient employees in any field can go terribly wrong – or incredibly right.

Imagine the cashier who is always early, bright-eyed, cheerful, moving through transactions swiftly and steadily, all the while greeting customers warmly and crisply, up-selling enthusiastically, answering customer questions accurately and concisely, and solving customer problems whenever they arise, and, when there are no customers waiting, keeping everything clean and organized behind the counter, jumping in to help others, and always watching that counter in case there is a customer approaching.

Think about it. Even if the cashier can operate the cash register and make correct change, there is a big difference between a cashier who is always a little bit early to work and doesn't take long breaks and one who is chronically late or disappears for long stretches of time. There is a big difference between the cashier who is bright-eyed and the one who is bleary-eyed; the one who is smiling and the one with the perpetual eye roll; the one who can help a customer when something is wrong with an order and one who is clueless; the one who is staring at their device, talking with peers behind the counter and the one who pays attention to the customer; the one who mumbles and the one who says enthusiastically, "Would you like a beverage today, sir?"

These differences may not be thrilling and sexy, but they matter. So much! They matter to your customers, to your vendors, to that employee's coworkers, to you and every other manager, and these differences have a huge impact on the bottom line. Yes, your employees (of all ages) must have the hard skills to do the job, but the soft skills make all the difference – whether at the lowest end of the technical skill spectrum or the highest.

Of course, some technical skills are in much greater demand and shorter supply – notably in the STEM (science, technology, engineering, and math) fields – mostly because they require a substantial amount of education and training. It's a whole lot more difficult and time-consuming to learn how to be a nurse than it is to learn how to operate the cash register. Employers in health care, computing, software, hardware, accounting, finance, and other "talent wars" industries need to hire people who have gone to the time and trouble and cost on their own initiative to acquire these in-demand technical skills for these higher-end jobs. That's why these employers are always scrambling to find enough "qualified" talent. While it's very difficult for these employers to place a real premium on soft skills for very in-demand hard skill jobs, the soft skills are even more important at the high end:

◆ Even if the nurse got straight As in nursing school and is great at, say, inserting needles and tubes into the human body, if that nurse falls asleep on the night shift or forgets to note correctly when medicine has been given or does not communicate effectively, then patients will suffer and someone might die.

◆ Even if the network systems administrators know the hardware and software and all the crisscrossing cables, if they fail to do timely updates, or monitor storage capacity, or recognize patterns in user issues, the system might crash and burn.

◆ Even if the computer programmer can write great code very fast, if that programmer cannot understand the needs and objectives of business owners and users, that programmer is going to write a lot of great code to nowhere.

◆ Even if the data analyst is a master of collection, processing, and reporting, if the analyst doesn't work at a steady pace, gets distracted easily, and doesn't follow through in a timely manner on key deliverables, the leadership will be starved of key performance indicators and the enterprise could be going down the drain before anybody sees it coming.

◆ Even if the engineer can design, develop, and test devices of all shapes and sizes, if that engineer refuses to coordinate with other team members by doing the necessary reporting in the project management system; or cuts out early and puts extra work on the rest of the team; or smells bad or sneers or curses at colleagues, there will be stress and conflict on the team.

◆ Even if accountants know the audit process like the back of their hand, if they do not pay close attention to detail, or overlook details rather than having a difficult conversation, or reveal confidential company information on social media, someone could go to jail.

In our work, I've seen every one of these scenarios played out in the real world. Trust me. Soft skills matter. A lot! They are not trivial. Soft skills make the difference every day between life and death; between success and failure.

> Imagine the nurse who not only stays late and takes very few breaks, but whom patients know by name and trust and look forward to seeing; who sees more patients, spends more time with patients, knows more patients by name, and smiles at more patients; notices subtle changes and recognizes important symptoms even when they are not conspicuous; can give a patient or their family a greater feeling of dignity, safety, comfort, and motivation – not just medicine.

Here's what's really thrilling: Soft skills can also make the difference between mediocre and good; between good and great; between great and "one of a kind."

Just as I've seen the costly downsides of the soft skills gap, in our work, I've seen example after example proving the incredible power of soft skills. When you combine the necessary hard skills of a job with the right soft skills, the added value is so much more than the sum of its parts. The soft skills are like a supersonic jet fuel that magnifies the scope and quality of every stitch of work.

I promise you, this does not happen by accident.

Drill Down: The Missing Basics

Up to this point, I've been using the term "soft skills," as it is generally understood, to refer to the entire array of nontechnical skills.

Our soft skills model is focused on the most important "missing basics" – 12 specific skills – boiled down after studying the tens of thousands of details of behavior documented in our decades of research and training. These 12 missing basics are organized within three larger categories – professionalism, critical thinking, and teamwork.

Here's the model:

#1 Professionalism: The Missing Basics
◆ Self-evaluation: Regularly assessing your own thoughts, words, and actions against clear, meaningful standards; and your own performance against specific goals, timelines, guidelines, and parameters.
◆ Personal responsibility: Staying focused on what you can control directly – principally yourself – and controlling your responses in the face of factors outside your own control.
◆ Positive attitude: Maintaining and conveying a positive, generous, enthusiastic demeanor in your expressions, gestures, words, and tone.
◆ Good work habits: Wellness, self-presentation, timeliness, organization, productivity, quality, follow-through, and initiative.
◆ Interpersonal communication: Attentive listing, observing, and reading; perceiving and empathizing; effective use of words, tone, expressions and gestures – verbal, written, and otherwise, one-on-one and in groups, in-person and remotely.

#2 Critical Thinking: The Missing Basics
◆ Proactive learning: Keeping an open mind, suspending judgment, questioning assumptions, and seeking out information, technique, and perspective; and studying, practicing, and contemplating in order to build your stored knowledge base, skill set, and wisdom.
◆ Problem solving: Mastering established best practices –proven repeatable solutions for dealing with regular recurring decisions – so as to avoid reinventing the wheel. Using repeatable solutions to improvise when addressing decisions that are new but similar.
◆ Decision making: Identifying and considering multiple options, assessing the pros and cons of each, and choosing the course of action closest to the desired outcome.

#3 Teamwork: The Missing Basics
◆ Appreciating context: Reading and adapting to the existing structure, rules, customs, and leadership in an unfamiliar situation.

- Citizenship: Accepting, embracing, and observing, not just the rights and rewards, but the duties of membership/belonging/ participation in a defined group with its own structure, rules, customs, and leadership.
- Service: Approaching relationships in terms of what you have to offer – respect, commitment, hard work, creativity, sacrifice – rather than what you need or want.
- Playing your position: Doing the part assigned (or relegated) to you to support the larger mission; coordinating, cooperating, and collaborating with others in pursuit of a shared goal; supporting and celebrating the success of others.

As you read and reread the descriptions of the missing basics, you should be asking yourself:

- What are the highest-priority behaviors for your organization, for your team, for different roles on your team, for the various individuals on your team, and for you?
- Which behaviors are crucial to success?
- Which ones offer the greatest potential to increase competitive differentiation?

Imagine the network systems administrator who not only keeps the hardware and software running and updates systems, but tracks recurring user issues, finds root causes, and implements systemic solutions to recurring problems; not just maintaining storage, but exploring the cloud or some other innovation; not just a "manager" in title only, but a highly engaged leader who is coaching the other system administrators and technicians on the team.

Unlocking the Power of Soft Skills

Show me an organization with a strong, positive corporate culture and I will show you an organization that is very clear about exactly which soft skill behaviors are high priority – and often sings about those very behaviors from the rooftops. They don't just focus on their talent, of course, but their emphasis on key soft skill behaviors makes everybody in the organization much better – even the youngest, least experienced employees. To make it easy for you to picture, I'll ask you to picture the United States Marine Corps, or Disney. Both organizations, in very different lines of work, famously imbue a huge number of the soft skill behaviors in their workforce. There are many other examples:

- There is a quick-service restaurant chain that stands out as the very best in every single market in which they operate. Their employees, from top to bottom, of all ages, are always super clean-cut, wearing tidy uniforms, prompt and attentive, excessively polite, and always going the extra mile to ensure quality and service. I always jokingly reference Ned Flanders from *The Simpsons* – the "goody-goody" next-door neighbor – when I'm describing the personnel in this organization. Everybody who works there is like Ned Flanders. The organization is surely not a model of diversity, but it is a model of incredible soft skills throughout the organization. Whether you like Ned Flanders or not, you could see how he would do a great job in a role where what matters most is cleanliness, fresh hot food, and great customer service. Right?

- On the other end of the spectrum, there is a lunch concession in New York City near Wall Street where everything is made to order – but with lightning speed – that customers must learn to be prepared to order without delay in staccato fashion – "wheat bread, mayonnaise, turkey, muenster cheese, lettuce, tomato, onion" and with barely a pause the guy behind the counter is handing the customer a sandwich wrapped and marked – as the endless line moves swiftly and steadily past a self-service soup selection and beverage refrigerator – toward the cashier. If you don't move fast, you miss your opportunities, as the line just keeps moving. Their culture is all about pace (and consistently healthy portions). Customers know exactly what to expect – a very big sandwich, customized 100%, plus soup and a drink, all very fast. The place is a gold mine.

- There is a rental car chain that is consistently rated the best and also has been the most profitable and fastest growing for years on end. Why? Self-presentation. Quality. Teamwork. Initiative. Problem solving.

♦ There is a health care system where key metrics – wait time in emergency rooms, cost per care incident, safety, patient satisfaction, etc. – far surpass those of comparable hospitals. The reason is their incessant focus on a handful of high-priority behaviors among health care delivery personnel: Pace. Quality. Decision making. Teamwork. Service.

These powerful corporate cultures don't just happen. They are the result of an organization that knows exactly what its high-priority behaviors are, focuses on them relentlessly, and systematically drives those behaviors throughout the organization in all of its human capital management practices. When it works, it really works.

> Imagine the computer programmer who not only writes great code very fast, but also conducts in-depth interviews with business owners and users before, during, and after every key step in the development process, in order to better understand their needs and issues.

To be clear, these organizations do not necessarily use the same terms for key behaviors as they are named and described in our competency model. But if you drill down, you will see the same key soft skill behaviors recurring over and over again, underpinning these powerful cultures.

Most organizations with powerful cultures develop their own salient language and symbols – slogans and logos – internally and externally. Of course, the best organizations align their employer branding with their branding in the consumer marketplace. Slogans and logos – branding – with compelling messages are an important part of creating the shared meaning in an organization that helps define the culture. But it takes a whole lot more than slogans and logos to drive a powerful culture.

I've worked with some organizations that are all talk and no action when it comes to culture. They have great slogans, but they do not drive and support and reward key behaviors among employees that are in alignment with the messages. When employees have regular run-ins with customers because management has very strict policies against merchandise exchanges and returns, then it really doesn't matter how many placards there are in the store that say, "The customer is always right!" The slogans start to sound pretty empty.

I've also worked with organizations in which the leadership gets very serious about changing their corporate culture – all of a sudden. It's as if these leaders have an epiphany and realize what they've been missing and decide they want a strong, positive culture and they want it now. They want culture change overnight, by decree: "From now on, our culture will be _____!" Fill in the blank – "honesty!" "teamwork!" "innovation!" But you can't force culture change overnight. It takes time because behavior change takes time.

Imagine the data analyst who not only collects, processes, and reports data in a timely manner, but takes the initiative to report the data in more user-friendly formats so that they are easier to read and understand; to search for important patterns in the data; to extrapolate from those patterns to make meaningful predictions; and has the ability to make an effective verbal presentation to accompany the report.

Of course, there are also plenty of leaders who pay no attention to corporate culture whatsoever. I've had many senior executives tell me, "It was never an issue in the old days. Employees just did their jobs. Now that we have this generation gap, we are talking for the first time about our 'culture.'" I always tell these leaders, "Just because you have never paid any attention to culture doesn't mean you don't have a corporate culture. It just means you have a culture by default instead of by design." Every organization has a corporate culture. Your corporate culture is simply the combined web of prevailing shared beliefs, meaning, language, practices, and traditions that have developed over time between and among the people in your organization.

Take a few minutes to think: How would you describe the culture of your organization? What about your team? Are they aligned?

Is your culture by default or design?

> Imagine the engineer who not only designs, develops, and tests devices very well, very fast, but also checks every box on time at every step of the way in the project management system; is great at interpersonal communication; actively celebrates the success of others; and is always ready to sacrifice for the team.

Of course, you can't control the whole culture of your entire organization (unless, of course, you are the big, big boss). Still, whether you are the CEO or a manager with a small team, what you can control is your sphere – whatever part of the organization is your responsibility.

If your organization has a strong, positive culture by design, then you need to be in alignment. What are the high-priority behaviors? What are you doing in your sphere to drive and support and reward those behaviors in everything you do as a leader?

If your organization has a less than strong positive culture – or a culture by default – then it's all up to you. You need to create your own culture within your own sphere. You don't need to start a revolution. But you can be a little bit of a maverick. You can certainly be a change leader. Believe me: Your results will speak for themselves – your team will stand out, not just in its business outcomes, but in cohesiveness, morale, and retention.

What are the high-priority behaviors that are most important in your sphere? Crucial to success? Or jet fuel for competitive differentiation? Make them the foundation of your culture. Focus on them relentlessly, and systematically drive those behaviors throughout your sphere in all of your human capital management practices. Develop your own salient language and symbols – slogans and logos. Make sure it aligns with your organization's "brand." Then sing it from the rooftops – make it 1000% clear. And start doing everything within your power to drive and support and reward those high-priority behaviors in every employee within your sphere.

> Imagine the accountant who not only knows the rules, follows the rules, and helps clients follow the rules, but also has the guts and tact to talk clients through the difficult details and the savvy to help them ethically navigate around, over, under, or through; or maybe even has the initiative, creativity, and innovation to find a hidden opportunity or invent the next great loophole.

Unlocking the Power: The Rest of This Book

The rest of this book is dedicated to helping you teach the missing basics – complete with step-by-step lesson plans. Just imagine the impact you could have if you were to spend time every week systematically building up the soft skills of your team. You will send a powerful message, week by week. You will make them aware. You will make them care. You will help them learn the missing basics one by one – one exercise at a time. You will build them up and make them so much better.

PART TWO

TEACHING THE MISSING BASICS

Part Two of this book is dedicated to helping you teach the missing basics – complete with step-by-step lesson plans. The missing basics are organized into chapters based on these three larger old-fashioned categories:

- ◆ How to Teach the Missing Basics of Professionalism
- ◆ How to Teach the Missing Basics of Critical Thinking
- ◆ How to Teach the Missing Basics of Teamwork

All of the exercises within the lesson plans are exercises we have developed and tested over the years in our seminars following this basic teaching strategy:

- ◆ Make them aware: Name it and describe what the skill means to the organization, the team, and you as a manager.
- ◆ Make them care: Explore what the skill means to them.
- ◆ Sell it: Explain the "self-building" value of the skill.
- ◆ Break it down: Spell out exactly what they need to do, step-by-step.
- ◆ Make it easy: Use ready-made lessons and exercises.
- ◆ Get them involved: Give them "credit" for self-directed learning.
- ◆ Make it practical: Spotlight opportunities to practice on-the-job.
- ◆ Follow up with coaching-style feedback to reinforce the lessons whenever possible.

All of the lesson plans and exercises within each lesson plan are designed to be highly flexible and easy to use:

- They can be used as self-directed learning by any individual or group.
- They can be used to guide one-on-one discussions with direct reports or anybody you are coaching.
- They can be conducted in a classroom as written exercises or as group discussions.
- Almost all of them can be done easily inside of an hour within a team meeting or an extended one-on-one.
- Some exercises may be such a good fit for the needs of a particular individual or for your team as a whole that you may find yourself regularly returning to them over and over again.

Not every lesson or exercise is for every team or individual, of course. Feel free to modify any of the lessons to fit your needs.

Spend time every day or every week building up the soft skills of your team. Send a powerful message. Make them aware. Make them care. Help them learn the missing basics one by one – one exercise at a time. Build them up and make them better. They will be so glad you did. You will too! Not to mention every manager they ever have for the rest of their careers.

Chapter 4

Teaching the Missing Basics of Professionalism

Professionalism: The Missing Basics

- ◆ **Self-evaluation:** Regularly assessing your own thoughts, words, and actions against clear meaningful standards; and your own performance against specific goals, timelines, guidelines, and parameters.
- ◆ **Personal responsibility:** Staying focused on what you can control directly – principally yourself – and controlling your responses in the face of factors outside your own control.
- ◆ **Positive attitude:** Maintaining and conveying a positive, generous, enthusiastic demeanor in your expressions, gestures, words, and tone.
- ◆ **Good work habits:** Wellness, self-presentation, timeliness, organization, productivity, quality, follow-through, and initiative.
- ◆ **Interpersonal communication:** Attentive listening, observing, and reading; perceiving and empathizing; effective use of words, tone, expressions, and gestures – verbal, written, and otherwise; one-on-one and in groups; in-person and remotely.

Teaching Self-Evaluation

Self-evaluation: Regularly assessing your own thoughts, words, and actions – against clear, meaningful standards; and your own performance against specific goals, timelines, guidelines, and parameters.

BRIDGING THE GAP

Here is a profound truth I learned from my longtime karate teacher, mentor, and friend Master Frank Gorman: "The mirror is the best teacher."

That is not true, however, if you always like what you see. I don't mean this to seem like a retro anti-self-esteem movement "make-a-point" moment. But if you always like what you see in the mirror, then you are actually a narcissist per se. In order to use the mirror as a teacher, you must have an external objective standard against which to measure your reflection. I'm not talking about artistic beauty or saying one kind of reflection is "better" than another in any kind of absolute way. Even if you make up the objective standard yourself, the key is using that standard to measure future performance. Juxtaposition with a clear standard is a necessary component of any kind of productive evaluation – especially self-evaluation. Otherwise, self-evaluation turns into navel-gazing – solipsism – which is distorting due to its narrowing perspective and therefore leads straight to unconditional self-acceptance or paralyzing self-loathing. Neither drives learning and growth.

What does drive learning and growth?

Regular productive honest self-evaluation against clear standards. That is not only the fundamental building block for teaching/learning the rest of the self-management skills, but it is the fundamental building block for teaching/learning all of the soft skills not to mention every hard skill, and practically any other kind of significant learning and growth. When it comes to continuous improvement of any kind, self-evaluation is the beginning, middle, and end.

For that reason, most of the lesson plans and exercises throughout the rest of this book revolve around self-evaluation tools of various types.

Before you get into the lesson plans here, you might consider starting with some big-picture assessment tools – tools that profile personality types, interests, values, and/or communication style. Try to identify (and vet) several of them, the more the better.

Where can you find them? Your organization may own some already – ask someone in HR. Or you can look online – there are plenty you can find for free and many more for sale. You can find them in books. You can often find a consultant who will be happy to help. Or you can create one yourself without too much trouble based on any competency model or any list of traits, characteristics, behaviors, skills, or preferences.

There is an endless supply of reasonably easy to access off-the shelf tools, including:

◆ Probably the best-known personality profiling tool is the Myers-Briggs Type Indicator, which is a proprietary tool that separates people into 16 types based on how they take in information, how they make decisions, whether they draw energy from internal sources or external, and whether they prefer to keep issues open or move them toward closure.

◆ There is another personality profile I like very much – a model on what I would call the "groovy" end of the spectrum – called the Enneagram – which separates people into nine categories based on differences in what ultimately motivates a person on the deepest level.

◆ In the middle of the spectrum, there are many very interesting profiles of communication styles using different frameworks of evaluation – direct/indirect, rational/emotional, assertive/receptive, aggressive/passive/passive-aggressive/manipulative.

Most can now be done online with automated reporting. Or you can often print out an assessment (or buy a kit) so it can be done on paper with an old-fashioned pen. Some are best delivered verbally with an interviewer or counselor.

You don't have to choose which big-picture assessment tool is best because you should consider doing several different self-assessments, using several different models. Finding your "type" according to different models is great way to obtain multiple perspectives on yourself in very short order. One option is to take these assessments one at a time, maybe once a week for a while. In the intervening time between assessments, make an effort to digest the results and test-drive what you learn. The second option is a self-assessment boot camp, completing a series of self-assessments in a very short time frame. Either way, just the process of completing a self-evaluation tool usually has a significant impact and, of course, the results are usually quite illuminating, especially when you can consider the results from multiple models. Using the results as a tool for self-improvement with or without a coach will take it to higher level still.

This can be a very powerful lesson because it helps put specific language – for anybody – around "what makes them different" and where they fit in relation to others. People are often surprised that they can be described as a recognizable type. It can offer a huge dose of self-awareness in a very short period of time.

These tools are a great shortcut to jump-start anybody's path to greater self-awareness. The downside of these tools is they usually take for granted that your type is fixed – the idea is "this is who you are" and that's not going to change. That's one reason I so strongly advocate using several different models so at least people gain a wider perspective on "who they are."

Once anybody gets familiar and comfortable with self-assessments, often they find they like it. Sometimes they really catch the bug of one of the models (be it Myers-Briggs, DISC, the Enneagram, and so forth) – or maybe they catch the bug of self-assessment in general. Never forget, evaluation is the foundation of continuous improvement; self-evaluation is the foundation of self-improvement.

When you get in the habit of evaluation/assessment, you start measuring everything that matters. More and more organizations are integrating into their cultures a regular practice of "measuring." The question is: What are they in the habit of measuring? Too often what gets measured most is removed from what individuals feel they can actually control. So, the "numbers" they are always hearing about don't tell them very much about their own performance and the specific actions they themselves can take to improve.

When it comes to using self-evaluation to drive continuous improvement, the key is measuring concrete actions within the control of the individual. Once you get into the habit of regular self-evaluation, take it to the next level by getting in the habit of measuring all the concrete actions within your control – the ones that matter – every step of the way.

In other words, keep score for yourself of everything you actually do at work. Create your own self-evaluation tools to monitor, measure, and document everything you do – or even better, create your own self-evaluation tools:

- ◆ For every project, there should be a project plan, including every goal and deadline along the way, complete with guidelines and parameters for every goal. Use project plans as tools for ongoing self-evaluation.
- ◆ For every recurring task or responsibility, there should be standard operating procedures, complete with checklists. Use those standard operating procedures and checklists as tools for ongoing self-evaluation. Every step of the way, you can track your progress on every task, one "check" at a time.
- ◆ To measure activities, log every activity.
- ◆ To measure time, create schedules and time logs.

If you can get in the habit of using these kinds of self-evaluation tools to monitor your own performance – measuring your own concrete actions against clear, measurable goals – you will put yourself squarely on the path to continuous improvement. Scorekeeping will double as a great source of ongoing real-time documentation.

This is why you should really care about creating the habit of regular self-evaluation: Research studies show that what really drives learning and growth is real self-awareness through regular, productive, honest self-evaluation against clear standards. That is the fundamental building block for systematically learning any skill. Without measuring yourself against some yardstick, it is very hard to set meaningful concrete goals for improvement, much less monitor your progress on the way toward meeting those goals. If you want to run far, you should measure your distance. If you want to run fast, you should measure your distance over time. If you want to run smarter, you should measure your training regimen against established best practices. If you want to run for charity, then you need to measure how much money you raise. And so on.

The key is to get in the habit of doing regular self-evaluation against external standards to build greater self-awareness in yourself so that you can support your own learning and growth going forward. Remember, "The mirror is the best teacher," provided that you learn how to use the mirror to measure your own performance against concrete goals for improvement.

Self-Evaluation: Lesson Plan #1

Step One: Brainstorm: What does "self-evaluation" mean to you?

Step Two: Consider the following definition of "Self-evaluation": Regularly assessing your own thoughts, words, and actions – against clear meaningful standards; and your own performance against specific goals, timelines, guidelines and parameters." Brainstorm: Why is this approach in the best interests of the organization? Why is this approach in your best interests as an employee?

Why is that the key to self-evaluation?

Step Three: Can you think of examples of individuals – inside or outside of work – exemplifying this approach to regular self-evaluation? Can you describe the example in detail? What happened? Where? When? Who was involved?

Step Four: Can you think of examples of a time when you exemplified this approach to regular self-evaluation – inside or outside of work? Can you describe the example in detail? What happened? Where? When? Who else was involved?

Self-Evaluation: Lesson Plan #2 – Evaluating Yourself on Ability, Skill, and Will

Evaluate yourself, generally, in terms of your natural abilities, skills, and motivation.

Ability

♦ What are my natural strengths that are applicable to my current tasks and responsibilities and projects? How am I applying those strengths?

♦ What are my relative weaknesses? How can I better leverage my strengths? How can I better plan around, bolster, or otherwise mitigate my weaknesses?

Technical Skills

♦ What are my key technical skills applicable to my current tasks and responsibilities and projects? How am I applying those skills?

♦ What are my relative technical skill gaps? How can I better leverage my skills? How can I bridge those skill gaps?

Soft Skills

♦ What are my key soft skills applicable to my current tasks and responsibilities and projects? How am I applying those skills?

♦ What are my relative soft skill gaps? How can I better leverage my soft skills? How can I bridge those soft skill gaps?

Will/Motivation

♦ What is my current motivation level? High, medium, or low?

♦ In what areas inside or outside of work am I most motivated?

♦ What motivates me? What can I do to get more of what motivates me?

♦ What de-motivates me? What can I do to avoid those things that de-motivate me?

Self-Evaluation: Lesson Plan #3 – Evaluating Yourself on Productivity, Quality, and Behavior

Evaluate yourself generally in terms of the major dimensions of performance at work.

Productivity:
◆ Are you getting enough work done fast enough?
◆ What can you do to get more work done faster?
◆ Should you revisit your priorities?
◆ Do you need to focus your time better?
◆ Do you need to postpone low-priority activities?
◆ How can you eliminate time wasters?
◆ Do you need better time budgets?
◆ Do you need to make better plans?

Quality:
◆ Are you meeting or exceeding guidelines and specifications for your tasks and responsibilities?
◆ What can you do to improve the quality of your work?
◆ Do you need to pay closer attention to detail?
◆ Do you need to make better use of checklists?
◆ Do you need to start adding some bells and whistles to your work product?

Behavior:
◆ What can you do to make sure that your intangible behaviors are positive?
◆ Are there substandard behaviors you can eliminate? Which ones? How can you eliminate them?
◆ Are there superstar behaviors you can start adding? How can you eliminate them?
◆ Should you be taking more initiative or less?
◆ How can you take more initiative without overstepping your bounds?

Self-Evaluation: Lesson Plan #4 – Evaluating Yourself on the Key Soft Skills Competencies

For each of the 12 soft skills, answer the following questions.

When it comes to your natural abilities and inclinations:
◆ Is this a natural strength? Or is this a natural weakness?
 On a scale of 1 (weakest) to 10 (strongest)

When it comes to your learned skills:
◆ Is this a skill you've practiced and made strong? Or is this a weakness?
 On a scale of 1 (weakest) to 10 (strongest)

When it comes to your experience:
◆ Is this a skill in which you have gained a lot of experience? Or very little?
 On a scale of 1 (no experience) to 10 (extensive experience)

When it comes to your interest and motivation:
◆ Is this a skill in which you are interested and motivated?
 On a scale of 1 (not interested) to 10 (extremely motivated)

The soft skill of . . . *Self-Evaluation*: Regularly assessing your own thoughts, words, and actions against clear meaningful standards; and your own performance against specific goals, timelines, guidelines, and parameters.

On a scale of 1 (weakest) to 10 (strongest):

◆ Is this a natural strength? Or is this a natural weakness?
◆ Is this a skill you've actively studied and practiced? Or not?
◆ Is this a skill with which you have a lot of experience? Or not?
◆ Is this a skill in which you are highly motivated? Or not?

The soft skill of . . . *Personal Responsibility*: Staying focused on what you can control directly – principally yourself – and controlling your responses in the face of factors outside your own control.

On a scale of 1 (weakest) to 10 (strongest):

- Is this a natural strength? Or is this a natural weakness?
- Is this a skill you've actively studied and practiced? Or not?
- Is this a skill with which you have a lot of experience? Or not?
- Is this a skill in which you are highly motivated? Or not?

The soft skill of . . . *Positive Attitude:* Maintaining and conveying a positive, generous, enthusiastic demeanor in your expressions, gestures, words, and tone.

On a scale of 1 (weakest) to 10 (strongest):

- Is this a natural strength? Or is this a natural weakness?
- Is this a skill you've actively studied and practiced? Or not?
- Is this'a skill with which you have a lot of experience? Or not?
- Is this a skill in which you are highly motivated? Or not?

The soft skill of . . . *Good Work Habits*: Wellness, self-presentation, timeliness, organization, productivity, quality, follow-through, and initiative.

On a scale of 1 (weakest) to 10 (strongest):

- Is this a natural strength? Or is this a natural weakness?
- Is this a skill you've actively studied and practiced? Or not?
- Is this a skill with which you have a lot of experience? Or not?
- Is this a skill in which you are highly motivated? Or not?

The soft skill of . . . *Interpersonal Communication*: Attentive listening, observing, and reading; perceiving and empathizing; effective use of words, tone, expressions and gestures – verbal, written, and otherwise; one-on-one and in groups; in-person and remotely.

On a scale of 1 (weakest) to 10 (strongest):

- Is this a natural strength? Or is this a natural weakness?
- Is this a skill you've actively studied and practiced? Or not?

◆ Is this a skill with which you have a lot of experience? Or not?
◆ Is this a skill in which you are highly motivated? Or not?

The soft skill of . . . *Proactive Learning*: Keeping an open mind, suspending judgment, questioning assumptions; seeking out information, technique, and perspective; and studying, practicing, and contemplating in order to build your stored knowledge base, skillset, and wisdom.

On a scale of 1 (weakest) to 10 (strongest):

◆ Is this a natural strength? Or is this a natural weakness?
◆ Is this a skill you've actively studied and practiced? Or not?
◆ Is this a skill with which you have a lot of experience? Or not?
◆ Is this a skill in which you are highly motivated? Or not?

The soft skill of . . . *Problem Solving*: Mastering established best practices – proven, repeatable solutions for dealing with regular recurring decisions – so as to avoid reinventing the wheel. Using repeatable solutions to improvise when addressing decisions that are new but similar.

On a scale of 1 (weakest) to 10 (strongest):

◆ Is this a natural strength? Or is this a natural weakness?
◆ Is this a skill you've actively studied and practiced? Or not?
◆ Is this a skill with which you have a lot of experience? Or not?
◆ Is this a skill in which you are highly motivated? Or not?

The soft skill of . . . *Decision Making*: Identifying and considering multiple options, assessing the pros and cons of each, and choosing the course of action closest to the desired outcome.

On a scale of 1 (weakest) to 10 (strongest):

◆ Is this a natural strength? Or is this a natural weakness?
◆ Is this a skill you've actively studied and practiced? Or not?
◆ Is this a skill with which you have a lot of experience? Or not?
◆ Is this a skill in which you are highly motivated? Or not?

The soft skill of . . . *Respect for Context*: Reading and adapting to the existing structure, rules, customs, and leadership in an unfamiliar situation.

On a scale of 1 (weakest) to 10 (strongest):

- Is this a natural strength? Or is this a natural weakness?
- Is this a skill you've actively studied and practiced? Or not?
- Is this a skill with which you have a lot of experience? Or not?
- Is this a skill in which you are highly motivated? Or not?

The soft skill of . . . *Good Citizenship*: Accepting, embracing, and observing, not just the rights and rewards, but also the duties of membership/belonging in a defined group with its own structure, rules, customs, and leadership.

On a scale of 1 (weakest) to 10 (strongest):

- Is this a natural strength? Or is this a natural weakness?
- Is this a skill you've actively studied and practiced? Or not?
- Is this a skill with which you have a lot of experience? Or not?
- Is this a skill in which you are highly motivated? Or not?

The soft skill of . . . *Service*: Approaching relationships in terms of what you have to offer – respect, commitment, hard work, creativity, sacrifice – rather than what you need or want.

On a scale of 1 (weakest) to 10 (strongest):

- Is this a natural strength? Or is this a natural weakness?
- Is this a skill you've actively studied and practiced? Or not?
- Is this a skill with which you have a lot of experience? Or not?
- Is this a skill in which you are highly motivated? Or not?

The soft skill of . . . *Teamwork*: Doing the part assigned (or relegated) to you to support the larger mission; coordinating, cooperating, and collaborating with others in pursuit of a shared goal; supporting and celebrating the success of others.

On a scale of 1 (weakest) to 10 (strongest):

- Is this a natural strength? Or is this a natural weakness?
- Is this a skill you've actively studied and practiced? Or not?
- Is this a skill with which you have a lot of experience? Or not?
- Is this a skill in which you are highly motivated? Or not?

Self-Evaluation: Lesson Plan #5 – Drill Down on Understanding the Key Soft Skills Competencies

For each of the 12 soft skills, answer the following questions.

- ◆ Can you think of a person whom you believe to be highly effective at this skill?
- ◆ Can you think of an example you've witnessed of this skill in action? Can you describe it? What makes this skill in action so valuable? What do you learn from this?

The soft skill of . . . *Self-Evaluation*: Regularly assessing your own thoughts, words, and actions against clear meaningful standards; and your own performance against specific goals, timelines, guidelines, and parameters.

- ◆ Can you think of a person whom you believe to be highly effective at this skill?
- ◆ Can you think of an example you've witnessed of this skill in action? Can you describe it? What makes this skill in action so valuable? What do you learn from this?

The soft skill of . . . *Personal Responsibility*: Staying focused on what you can control directly – principally yourself – and controlling your responses in the face of factors outside your own control.

- ◆ Can you think of a person whom you believe to be highly effective at this skill?
- ◆ Can you think of an example you've witnessed of this skill in action? Can you describe it? What makes this skill in action so valuable? What do you learn from this?

The soft skill of . . . *Positive Attitude*: Maintaining and conveying a positive, generous, enthusiastic demeanor in your expressions, gestures, words, and tone.

- ◆ Can you think of a person whom you believe to be highly effective at this skill?

◆ Can you think of an example you've witnessed of this skill in action? Can you describe it? What makes this skill in action so valuable? What do you learn from this?

The soft skill of . . . *Good Work Habits*: Wellness, self-presentation, timeliness, organization, productivity, quality, follow-through, and initiative.

◆ Can you think of a person whom you believe to be highly effective at this skill?
◆ Can you think of an example you've witnessed of this skill in action? Can you describe it? What makes this skill in action so valuable? What do you learn from this?

The soft skill of . . . *Interpersonal Communication*: Attentive listening, observing, and reading; perceiving and empathizing; effective use of words, tone, expressions, and gestures – verbal, written, and otherwise; one-on-one and in groups; in-person and remotely.

◆ Can you think of a person whom you believe to be highly effective at this skill?
◆ Can you think of an example you've witnessed of this skill in action? Can you describe it? What makes this skill in action so valuable? What do you learn from this?

The soft skill of . . . *Proactive Learning*: Keeping an open mind, suspending judgment, questioning assumptions; seeking out information, technique, and perspective; and studying, practicing, and contemplating in order to build your stored knowledge base, skillset, and wisdom.

◆ Can you think of a person whom you believe to be highly effective at this skill?
◆ Can you think of an example you've witnessed of this skill in action? Can you describe it? What makes this skill in action so valuable? What do you learn from this?

The soft skill of . . . *Problem Solving*: Mastering established best practices – proven, repeatable solutions for dealing with regular recurring decisions – so as to avoid reinventing the wheel. Using repeatable solutions to improvise when addressing decisions that are new but similar.

- ◆ Can you think of a person whom you believe to be highly effective at this skill?
- ◆ Can you think of an example you've witnessed of this skill in action? Can you describe it? What makes this skill in action so valuable? What do you learn from this?

The soft skill of . . . *Decision Making*: Identifying and considering multiple options, assessing the pros and cons of each, and choosing the course of action closest to the desired outcome.

- ◆ Can you think of a person whom you believe to be highly effective at this skill?
- ◆ Can you think of an example you've witnessed of this skill in action? Can you describe it? What makes this skill in action so valuable? What do you learn from this?

The soft skill of . . . *Respect for Context*: Reading and adapting to the existing structure, rules, customs, and leadership in an unfamiliar situation.

- ◆ Can you think of a person whom you believe to be highly effective at this skill?
- ◆ Can you think of an example you've witnessed of this skill in action? Can you describe it? What makes this skill in action so valuable? What do you learn from this?

The soft skill of . . . *Good Citizenship*: Accepting, embracing, and observing, not just the rights and rewards, but also the duties of membership/belonging in a defined group with its own structure, rules, customs, and leadership.

- ◆ Can you think of a person whom you believe to be highly effective at this skill?

♦ Can you think of an example you've witnessed of this skill in action? Can you describe it? What makes this skill in action so valuable? What do you learn from this?

The soft skill of . . . *Service*: Approaching relationships in terms of what you have to offer – respect, commitment, hard work, creativity, sacrifice – rather than what you need or want.

♦ Can you think of a person whom you believe to be highly effective at this skill?
♦ Can you think of an example you've witnessed of this skill in action? Can you describe it? What makes this skill in action so valuable? What do you learn from this?

The soft skill of . . . *Teamwork*: Doing the part assigned (or relegated) to you to support the larger mission; coordinating, cooperating, and collaborating with others in pursuit of a shared goal; supporting and celebrating the success of others.

♦ Can you think of a person whom you believe to be highly effective at this skill?
♦ Can you think of an example you've witnessed of this skill in action? Can you describe it? What makes this skill in action so valuable? What do you learn from this?

Self-Evaluation: Lesson Plan #6 – Explore Your Own Successes with the Key Soft Skills

For each of the 12 soft skills, answer the following questions:

◆ Can you think of a time when you've been successful with this skill in action? Describe what happened. When? Where? Who else was involved?

◆ What lessons do you take away from this experience? How could you improve when it comes to this skill? What is your next step?

The soft skill of . . . *Self-Evaluation*: Regularly assessing your own thoughts, words, and actions against clear meaningful standards; and your own performance against specific goals, timelines, guidelines, and parameters.

◆ Can you think of a time when you've been successful with this skill in action? Describe what happened. When? Where? Who else was involved?

◆ What lessons do you take away from this experience? How could you improve when it comes to this skill? What is your next step?

The soft skill of . . . *Personal Responsibility*: Staying focused on what you can control directly – principally yourself – and controlling your responses in the face of factors outside your own control.

◆ Can you think of a time when you've been successful with this skill in action? Describe what happened. When? Where? Who else was involved?

◆ What lessons do you take away from this experience? How could you improve when it comes to this skill? What is your next step?

The soft skill of . . . *Positive Attitude*: Maintaining and conveying a positive, generous, enthusiastic demeanor in your expressions, gestures, words, and tone.

♦ Can you think of a time when you've been successful with this skill in action? Describe what happened. When? Where? Who else was involved?

♦ What lessons do you take away from this experience? How could you improve when it comes to this skill? What is your next step?

The soft skill of . . . *Good Work Habits*: Wellness, self-presentation, timeliness, organization, productivity, quality, follow-through, and initiative.

♦ Can you think of a time when you've been successful with this skill in action? Describe what happened. When? Where? Who else was involved?

♦ What lessons do you take away from this experience? How could you improve when it comes to this skill? What is your next step?

The soft skill of . . . *Interpersonal Communication*: Attentive listening, observing, and reading; perceiving and empathizing; effective use of words, tone, expressions, and gestures – verbal, written, and otherwise; one-on-one and in groups; in-person and remotely.

♦ Can you think of a time when you've been successful with this skill in action? Describe what happened. When? Where? Who else was involved?

♦ What lessons do you take away from this experience? How could you improve when it comes to this skill? What is your next step?

The soft skill of . . . *Proactive Learning*: Keeping an open mind, suspending judgment, questioning assumptions; seeking out information, technique, and perspective; and studying, practicing, and contemplating in order to build your stored knowledge base, skillset, and wisdom.

- ◆ Can you think of a time when you've been successful with this skill in action? Describe what happened. When? Where? Who else was involved?
- ◆ What lessons do you take away from this experience? How could you improve when it comes to this skill? What is your next step?

The soft skill of . . . *Problem Solving*: Mastering established best practices – proven, repeatable solutions for dealing with regular recurring decisions – so as to avoid reinventing the wheel. Using repeatable solutions to improvise when addressing decisions that are new but similar.

- ◆ Can you think of a time when you've been successful with this skill in action? Describe what happened. When? Where? Who else was involved?
- ◆ What lessons do you take away from this experience? How could you improve when it comes to this skill? What is your next step?

The soft skill of . . . *Decision Making*: Identifying and considering multiple options, assessing the pros and cons of each, and choosing the course of action closest to the desired outcome.

- ◆ Can you think of a time when you've been successful with this skill in action? Describe what happened. When? Where? Who else was involved?
- ◆ What lessons do you take away from this experience? How could you improve when it comes to this skill? What is your next step?

The soft skill of . . . *Respect for Context*: Reading and adapting to the existing structure, rules, customs, and leadership in an unfamiliar situation.

- ◆ Can you think of a time when you've been successful with this skill in action? Describe what happened. When? Where? Who else was involved?

- What lessons do you take away from this experience? How could you improve when it comes to this skill? What is your next step?

The soft skill of . . . *Good Citizenship*: Accepting, embracing, and observing, not just the rights and rewards, but also the duties of membership/belonging in a defined group with its own structure, rules, customs, and leadership.

- Can you think of a time when you've been successful with this skill in action? Describe what happened. When? Where? Who else was involved?
- What lessons do you take away from this experience? How could you improve when it comes to this skill? What is your next step?

The soft skill of . . . *Service*: Approaching relationships in terms of what you have to offer – respect, commitment, hard work, creativity, sacrifice – rather than what you need or want.

- Can you think of a time when you've been successful with this skill in action? Describe what happened. When? Where? Who else was involved?
- What lessons do you take away from this experience? How could you improve when it comes to this skill? What is your next step?

The soft skill of . . . *Teamwork*: Doing the part assigned (or relegated) to you to support the larger mission; coordinating, cooperating, and collaborating with others in pursuit of a shared goal; supporting and celebrating the success of others.

- Can you think of a time when you've been successful with this skill in action? Describe what happened. When? Where? Who else was involved?
- What lessons do you take away from this experience? How could you improve when it comes to this skill? What is your next step?

Teaching Personal Responsibility

Personal responsibility: Staying focused on what you can control directly – principally your own thoughts, words, and actions – and controlling your responses in the face of factors outside your own control.

BRIDGING THE GAP

Here is the reality: In any situation, there are factors beyond our control. For example, I feel gravity and time are constantly holding me back! And in any situation there are factors within our control: our own thoughts, words, and actions. Almost anyone can focus on those outside factors or those inside factors. In fact, there is a lot of evidence to suggest that most people – of all ages – have a tendency to point to outside factors beyond the control of the individual when explaining their own shortcomings and failures, not to mention the successes of others. Funny enough, most people also have a strong tendency to point to factors within the direct control of the individual when it comes to our own successes as well as the failures and shortcomings of others. So at least the good news is that most people know how to focus on factors within the control of the individual. It's just that we take our focus off those factors when we make excuses, blame others, and complain.

When it comes to teaching personal responsibility, the key is keeping the focus on factors within the control of the individual. Teach them to ask themselves every step of the way: What is within my control right now? Where will I focus my attention and energy? What are my options? What's the plan? What are my next steps? What are my next thoughts, words, and actions?

This is why you should really care about increasing your sense of personal responsibility. No matter how high or low your position, if you focus your attention and energy on factors outside your control, you will render yourself "powerless," by definition. However, the flip side is also true. No matter how high or low your position, if you focus your attention and energy on factors within your control, you will maximize your power. In any situation, no matter how little is within your control, the way to make yourself more powerful is to focus like a laser beam on whatever thoughts, words, and actions you can take – your choices and the effects you can cause. Sometimes it is a very small amount of power – but more power is better than less power.

The key is learning to ask yourself every step of the way: "What is within my control right now? Where will I focus my attention and energy? What are my options? What's the plan? What are my next steps? What are my next thoughts, words, and actions?" That's how you increase your "response-power" in any situation."

Personal Responsibility: Lesson Plan #1 – Introduction

Step One: Brainstorm: What does "personal responsibility" mean to you?

Step Two: Consider the following definition of "personal responsibility": "Staying focused on what you can control directly – principally your own thoughts, words, and actions – and controlling your responses in the face of factors outside your own control." Brainstorm: Why is this approach to personal responsibility in the best interests of the organization? Why is this approach to personal responsibility in your best interests as an employee? Why is that the key to personal responsibility?

Step Three: Can you think of examples of individuals – inside or outside of work – exemplifying this approach to personal responsibility? Can you describe the example in detail? What happened? Where? When? Who was involved?

Step Four: Can you think of examples of a time when you exemplified this approach to personal responsibility – inside or outside of work? Can you describe the example in detail? What happened? Where? When? Who else was involved?

Personal Responsibility: Lesson Plan #2 – All the Factors That Get in Your Way

Step One: Brainstorm all of the factors that get in the way of your ability to do your job and make it harder for you to perform at the highest level.

Step Two: Now take a look at all the factors you've listed and ask yourself for each factor, "Is this a factor within my control or outside my control?" Take note of how many are within and how many are outside your control. What is the score?

Step Three: Consider any one (or all) of the factors you've listed above:

- ◆ Describe a recent example. Exactly how did this factor get in your way? When? Where? Who was involved? What happened?
- ◆ Now ask yourself: What did you do? What could you have done differently in retrospect? What were your options? What thoughts, words, and actions could you have changed?
- ◆ Now look ahead: Can you anticipate this factor getting in your way in the future? When is that likely to happen? Where? Who might be involved? What do you think is likely to happen? How will you respond? What options will you have? What thoughts, words, and/or actions are available to you? What can you do to improve the outcome?

Personal Responsibility: Lesson Plan #3 – Considering the Most Common Factors, Mostly Outside Your Own Control, That Get in the Way at Work

Step One: Consider the most common factors that people in the workplace commonly list as factors, mostly outside their own control, when asked to brainstorm factors that get in their way at work.

- ◆ Resource constraints – insufficient information, people, material, or tools
- ◆ Limited time
- ◆ Too much work
- ◆ Other people not doing their part
- ◆ Things are constantly changing
- ◆ Competing priorities
- ◆ Distance
- ◆ Weather
- ◆ Company policies, rules, regulations, and procedures
- ◆ The way things have always been done around here
- ◆ Too many low-priority distractions
- ◆ Interruptions
- ◆ Conflict between and among employees
- ◆ My manager is often unavailable
- ◆ Unclear lines of authority
- ◆ I answer to too many different people
- ◆ Inconsistency from one manager to another

Step Two: Consider any (or all) of the factors above. For each one that resonates with you:

- ◆ Describe a recent example. Exactly how did this factor get in your way? When? Where? Who was involved? What happened?
- ◆ Now ask yourself: What did you do? What could you have done differently in retrospect? What were your options? What thoughts, words, and actions could you have changed?

◆ Now look ahead: Can you anticipate this factor getting in your way in the future? When is that likely to happen? Where? Who might be involved? What do you think is likely to happen? How will you respond? What options will you have? What thoughts, words, and/or actions are available to you? What can you do to improve the outcome?

Personal Responsibility: Lesson Plan #4 – Response Power

Step One: Learn to use the "response power" mantra: Focus on the list of problems or obstacles that get in your way at work. Now take those items on your list, one by one, and practice applying the "response power" mantra: "What's outside my control? What's inside my control? (My own thoughts, words, actions) What are my options? What are my next steps?"

Step Two: Learn to use this simple tool to go along with the "response power" mantra.

For any situation, simply arrange those questions in a horizontal axis at the top of a page, to make vertical columns, and then fill in your answers side by side.

Outside	Inside (my own thoughts, words, actions)	Options?	Next Steps?

Step Three: Practice using the mantra and tool.

- Choose a factor outside your control that you can anticipate getting in your way in the near future.
- Now apply the mantra and the tool to think through in advance and prepare:
- Ask yourself:
  - What's outside my control?
  - What's inside my control? (My own thoughts, words, actions)
  - What are my options?
  - What are my next steps?"

Step Four: Consider the question, "What about those times when there really is nothing you can do?"

- Consider the following: If there is really "nothing" you can do, then why are you still thinking about it? Why are you still talking about it? Focus on something you CAN do.

Step Five: HOMEWORK. Use "response power" – the mantra and the tool – whenever it is appropriate going forward.

- ◆ What's outside my control?
- ◆ What's inside my control? (My own thoughts, words, actions)
- ◆ What are my options?
- ◆ What are my next steps?"

Teaching Positive Attitude

Positive attitude: Conveying optimism, generosity, support, and enthusiasm in your expressions, gestures, words, and tone.

BRIDGING THE GAP

There is no doubt that employee attitudes affect productivity, quality, morale; collegiality, cooperation, and cohesion; employee development; and retention as well as turnover. Good employee attitudes drive positive results. Bad employee attitudes put a drag on results. That's a fact proven by study after study, including our own.

Perhaps we are all being conditioned by social media to err on the side of oversharing our feelings. Displaying a good attitude is NOT all about what's going on deep inside. Instead, place the focus on external behavior; keep negative feelings on the inside and display positive expressions, gestures, words, and tone on the outside.

Do not make the three most common mistakes when dealing with "bad attitudes":

- Treating attitude as a personal issue, an "internal" state of mind that is off limits
- Treating attitude as unchangeable ("that's just who I am") matter of personality
- Talking about attitude in vague terms or indirectly

As long as you think of attitude as a personal, internal matter, it is going to remain intangible. Feelings are on the inside. Observable behavior is on the outside. That observable behavior can be seen, heard, and felt. No matter how intrinsic the source may be, it is only the external behavior that can be and must be managed. Dealing with attitude becomes a whole lot easier if you treat it head-on, directly, as just another matter of performance management. Here's my best advice:

- Make great attitude an explicit performance goal.
- Make it about external behaviors.
- Define the specific behaviors of great attitude: the expressions, words, tone, and gestures.
- Focus on the practice of displaying those specific behaviors.

This is why you should care about demonstrating a positive attitude at work. Attitude may be hard to define and describe – great, good, bad, or average. But it is very, very important. At every level, leaders and managers rate "attitude" as one of the most important factors in employee performance. Attitude can be the difference between success and failure for our business. Attitude can be the difference between success and failure for any employee.

Even so, many leaders and managers fail to talk about the power of attitude. Many believe that attitude is a personal issue and so it is off-limits. Many believe that attitude is just "who a person is" and can't be changed and so they don't try. Many believe attitude is vague and so they wouldn't know where to begin. Those beliefs are all wrong and that approach is a big mistake.

Here's the good news. Attitude is not a vague, internal matter that is unchangeable. Like anything else, displaying a positive attitude is a skillset that can be learned and mastered. Attitude is simply too important to leave off the table. So we are going to talk about it. We are going to focus on external behaviors. The bottom line is simple: Good attitudes are required. Not on the inside. What you feel on the inside is your business, 100%. But on the outside, positive words, tones, and gestures are required and expected. Here's some more good news. Research shows that if you make an effort to display positive words, tones, and gestures on the outside, it has a positive effect on your internal brain chemistry and actually makes you feel better on the inside.

Here's the bottom line. If you learn to display a positive attitude at work, regardless of what you are feeling inside, then you will have learned one of the most important broad transferable skills you could ever learn. You will be valued for your positive attitude in any role in any organization anywhere any time. And that is a skill that will never become obsolete.

Positive Attitude: Lesson Plan #1 – Considering Theories of How to Be Your Best at Work

There are a lot of theories out there about how to bring out the best attitudes in people at work. Consider these leading ideas.

- ◆ *Idea #1: Play to your strengths at work.* Work primarily on tasks and responsibilities that you enjoy and are particularly good at. The only problem is that most of us don't have that luxury.
  - *Brainstorming Question*: How do you keep doing good work day after day – and feel good about it – when the work is not necessarily work that you enjoy or excel at?
- ◆ *Idea #2: Balance your time at work with free time.* Rest, recover, relax, and rejuvenate in between times you must work. But the problem is that most of us simply don't have enough time to do everything we need to do each day, much less "free" time.
  - *Brainstorming Question*: How do you stay focused and energetic when you barely have time to think, much less rest?
- ◆ *Idea #3: Work with people you like and respect.* Avoid people you find "toxic" and stick to those you appreciate. The only problem is that very few people can choose their coworkers, subordinates, bosses, vendors, and customers.
  - *Brainstorming Question*: How do you maintain your equilibrium and equanimity when you have to deal with so many people you probably would not choose as your colleagues?
- ◆ *Idea #4: Work in a workspace that is comfortable and in a location that you enjoy.* If only!
  - *Brainstorming Question*: How do you stay upbeat and strong if you are physically uncomfortable at work and stuck in a location that is not your preference?
- ◆ *Idea #5: Leave your non-work issues at the door when you arrive at work.* The problem is: If things are adrift in your life outside of work, then you will be distracted by those concerns, whether you are at work or at home.
  - *Brainstorming Question*: How do you remain focused and positive at work when things might be problematic in your personal life?

Positive Attitude: Lesson Plan #2 – Defining "Good Attitude" Behaviors

Step One: Make a list. What does it mean to have a great attitude? Make a list of as many traits, characteristics, and behaviors you possibly can.

Step Two: Take the first item on your "good attitude" list: Break it down. Spell it out. Describe it. Describe it. Describe it some more.

Step Three: Take the remaining items on your "good attitude" list, one by one, and repeat the process from step two: Break it down. Spell it out. Describe, describe, describe.

Step Four: Consider your detailed descriptions of "good attitude" traits, characteristics, and behaviors. Now ask yourself: What are the recurring external behaviors you can identify? What are the recurring expressions, words, tones, and gestures?

Step Five: Considering what you've learned, how would you define "good attitude" in terms of observable measurable external behaviors?

Step Six: Consider whether these are behaviors that can be made performance goals? If so, how?

Positive Attitude: Lesson Plan #3 – Considering the Most Common Bad Attitudes

Everybody has bad days or bad moments. The purpose of this exercise is not to find out whether or not you have a bad attitude. The purpose is to figure out – when you do have bad days or bad moments – what kind of bad attitude behavior are you most likely to display? Armed with that information, you will be much better prepared to avoid that behavior and take corrective action more swiftly when it does happen.

Step One: Consider the most common aberrant communication practices in the workplace – otherwise known as "bad attitudes." When you are not at your best, which of these bad attitude behaviors are you most likely to display?

♦ Do you sometimes behave like a "porcupine"?
  Porcupines send the message: "Get away from me!"

♦ Do you sometimes behave like an "entangler"?
  Entanglers want everybody else to be involved in their issues – they want to be noticed, observed, listened to, and engaged – even if those issues are not the concern of the person in question.

♦ Do you sometimes behave like a "debater"?
  Debaters always have an argument to make, regardless of whether it is a good argument or not.

♦ Do you sometimes behave like a "complainer"?
  Complainers point out the negative symptoms of a situation without offering a solution based on the root cause.

♦ Do you sometimes behave like a "blamer"?
  Blamers are like complainers, pointing out negative symptoms, but blamers point the finger at a specific individual.

♦ Do you sometimes behave like a "stink bomb thrower"?
  Stink bomb throwers make sarcastic (or worse) remarks, curse under their breath (or aloud), or even make loud gestures such as slamming or yelling.

Step Two: Which bad attitude behaviors are you most likely to display? What does it look like? Specifically describe your behavior in those circumstances.

- ◆ Porcupines
- ◆ Entanglers
- ◆ Debaters
- ◆ Complainers
- ◆ Blamers
- ◆ Stink bomb throwers

What can you do to avoid behaving that way in the future? What can you do when you catch yourself behaving that way in the future to stop yourself?

Positive Attitude: Lesson Plan #4 – Considering Good Attitude Behaviors

Even if you have bad moments or bad days, of course you have plenty of good attitude in you. Everybody does. The purpose of this exercise is not to find out whether or not you have a good attitude. The purpose is to figure out – when you are at your best – what kinds of good attitude behaviors do you most often display? Armed with that information, you can try to leverage that strength with more purpose and consistency. Not only that, but you may become aware of other "good attitude" behaviors you would like to add to your repertoire!

Step One: Consider the most highly valued communication practices in the workplace – otherwise known as good attitudes. When you are at your best, which of these good attitude behaviors are you most likely to display?

- When you are at your best, are you approachable, welcoming, and professional?
- When you are at your best, do you communicate in a highly purposeful manner – brief, straightforward, and efficient?
- When you are at your best, do you choose your arguments carefully, and make your arguments based on clear evidence, rather than assertions of opinion?
- When you are at your best, are you a troubleshooter, placing the focus on what steps you can take yourself to make things better?
- When you are at your best, do you go out of your way to make positive, optimistic, generous comments? Speak in positive tones? Make positive gestures and expressions?

Step Two: Which good attitude behaviors are you most likely to display? What does it look like? Specifically describe your behavior in those circumstances.

- Being approachable, welcoming, and professional.
- Communicating in a highly purposeful manner – brief, straightforward, and efficient.

- ◆ Choosing your arguments carefully and basing them on clear evidence, rather than assertions of opinion.
- ◆ Troubleshooting, placing the focus on what steps you can take yourself to make things better.
- ◆ Making positive, optimistic, generous comments in positive tones, with positive gestures and expressions.

What can you do to leverage those strengths more in the future? What can you do to display other positive behaviors and leverage them as well?

Positive Attitude: Lesson Plan #5 – for Individuals Who Need an Attitude Adjustment

When you become aware of manifesting bad attitude behaviors, zero in on the issue and look for a replacement behavior.

Step One: Try to describe in detail the specific bad attitude behavior – the words, tones, expressions, and gestures. Instead of trying to perform psychoanalysis about the feelings on the inside, identify the specific negative behavior you want to stop.

Step Two: Connect the specific negative behavior to concrete negative outcomes you wish to avoid.

Step Three: Define a replacement behavior that you will use as a specific performance expectation against which to measure improvement.

Step Four: Monitor, measure, and document progress. Connect the specific improved behavior to specific positive outcomes. Celebrate success.

Teaching Good Work Habits

Good work habits: Self-presentation, timeliness, organization, productivity, quality, follow-through, consistency, and initiative.

BRIDGING THE GAP

Basic work habits are matters of "self-management," which has been a recurring theme in our work nearly since our research first began. That's because 99% of managers I've ever met would rather not have to do all the hard work of managing their direct reports, but instead deal with employees who pretty much manage themselves: "Do everything they are supposed to do when and how they are supposed to do it, on their own, without guidance, direction, or support." That's about as ridiculous as thinking that self-management means, "Do whatever you want, whenever you want, however you want."

Both of these versions of "self-management" are fantasyland. They are the poles on opposite ends of the soft skills gap.

Many people nowadays see basic work habits as matters of personal choice or style and often do not see the concrete business reasons for the requirements or preferences of their managers. On the other hand, sometimes managers have strong preferences or requirements for which there is no true business reason. That is the prerogative of the employer. After all, employers are paying employees, not the other way around. But our advice to managers is to choose your battles carefully on these issues. Every requirement (or preference) you impose on employees is one you will have to pay for somehow in the bargain; it is one less element of flexibility you will have to offer in the employment value proposition; or at least it is one less bargaining chip you have.

For the most part, there are very good reasons for following established best practices when it comes to work habits:

- When employees are unwell, there are increased health care costs and absenteeism, as well as diminished performance and impact on morale.
- When employees do not attend to their grooming and attire and manners, they make a negative impression on those with whom they interact.

- When employees come in late, take long breaks, leave early, and miss deadlines, they add less value and they keep other people waiting.
- When employees don't take notes, use checklists, or good systems of organization, they lose important information, lose track of what they are doing, and make it harder for others to coordinate with them.
- When employees don't pay attention to detail, they make more mistakes, causing diminished quality and requiring rework.
- When employees cannot be counted on to follow through, projects are left unfinished, and others are distracted and inconvenienced by having to remind them.
- When employees do not take initiative, opportunities are missed, and problems go unsolved.

These are all very strong business reasons. But not all of them apply to all people in all jobs. Before you choose to impose a requirement or preference when it comes to work habits, at least interrogate yourself: What are the business reasons? And what is the cost to you in terms of your flexibility in sweetening your employment proposition to your employees?

What really matters, in your case?

- When it comes to wellness:

- When it comes to self-presentation:

- When it comes to timeliness and employee work schedules:

- When it comes to meeting goals and deadlines:

- When it comes to using systems to stay organized:

- When it comes to paying attention to details:

- When it comes to follow-through:

- When it comes to taking initiative:

What really matters? If they really matter, they are worth learning and practicing.

Here's why you should care about learning best practices and building better work habits. These basic work habits might seem like matters of personal style or preference. But in fact there are strong business reasons for these requirements. How you present yourself and conduct yourself at work has a big impact on your performance and on everyone with whom you interact. Perhaps more to the point: It has a huge impact on your reputation at work.

Not following good work habits with consistency makes you seem younger and less mature. It gives some managers second thoughts about trusting you with important work. If you want to be taken seriously in the workplace, your best bet is to learn best practices and develop good work habits. People will perceive you as being more professional. That will be very much to your benefit, both in your current position and anywhere else you work.

Here is the big challenge. What makes this hard is that habits are habits for a reason. Habits feel good. Habits feel right. Even if you can see the logic for a different set of behaviors that will have better results, it is very hard to break one habit and create a new one. Research shows that it takes several weeks of consistent practice of a new set of behaviors to form a new habit. It takes even longer for a new habit to become entrenched. But remember, human beings are not just creatures of habit. We are products of our habits. Will you be the product of good habits or bad habits? That is your choice.

Good Work Habits: Lesson Plan #1 – Overview: Wellness, Self-Presentation, Timeliness, Productivity, Attention to Detail, Follow-Through, Initiative

Consider the following "work habits" and what they mean to you.

- *Wellness*: Maintaining a healthy body, mind, and spirit/mood.
  - *Brainstorming Question*: What are the business reasons for employers to have strong guidelines or requirements for employees when it comes to wellness? What are the reasons why it is in your best interests as an employee to follow best practices when it comes to wellness? Are there good reasons to NOT follow best practices when it comes to wellness?
- *Self-presentation*: Controlling your grooming, attire, and manners – given the social/cultural situation at hand – so as to make a positive impression on others.
  - *Brainstorming Question*: What are the business reasons for employers to have strong guidelines or requirements for employees when it comes to self-presentation? What are the reasons why it is in your best interests as an employee to follow best practices when it comes to self-presentation? Are there good reasons to NOT follow best practices when it comes to self-presentation?
- *Timeliness*: Arriving early, staying late, and taking short breaks. Meeting or beating schedules and deadlines.
  - *Brainstorming Question*: What are the business reasons for employers to have strong guidelines or requirements for employees when it comes to timeliness? What are the reasons why it is in your best interests as an employee to follow best practices when it comes to timeliness? Are there good reasons to NOT follow best practices when it comes to timeliness?
- *Productivity*: Working at a fast pace without significant interruptions.
  - *Brainstorming Question*: What are the business reasons for employers to have strong guidelines or requirements for employees when it comes to productivity? What are the reasons why it is in your best interests as an employee to follow best practices when it comes to productivity? Are there good

reasons to NOT follow best practices when it comes to productivity?

◆ *Organization*: Using proven systems for documentation and tracking – note-taking, project plans, checklists, and filing.

- *Brainstorming Question*: What are the business reasons for employers to have strong guidelines or requirements for employees when it comes to taking notes and using project plans, checklists, and filing systems? What are the reasons why it is in your best interests as an employee to follow best practices when it comes to taking notes and using project plans, checklists, and filing systems? Are there good reasons to NOT follow these best practices?

◆ *Attention to detail*: Following instructions, standard operating procedures, specifications, and staying focused and mindful in performing tasks and responsibilities.

- *Brainstorming Question*: What are the business reasons for employers to have strong guidelines or requirements for employees when it comes to attention to detail? What are the reasons why it is in your best interests as an employee to follow best practices when it comes to attention to detail? Are there good reasons to NOT follow best practices when it comes to paying attention to detail?

◆ *Follow-through and consistency*: Fulfilling your commitments and finishing what you start.

- *Brainstorming Question*: What are the business reasons for employers to have strong guidelines or requirements for employees when it comes to follow-through and consistency? What are the reasons why it is in your best interests as an employee to follow best practices when it comes to follow-through and consistency? Are there good reasons to NOT follow-through with consistency?

◆ *Initiative*: Self-starting. Taking productive action without explicit direction. Going above and beyond; the extra mile.

- *Brainstorming Question*: What are the business reasons for employers to have strong guidelines or requirements for employees when it comes to initiative? What are the reasons why it is in your best interests as an employee to follow best practices when it comes to initiative? Are there good reasons to NOT take initiative?

Good Work Habits: Lesson Plan #2 – Self-Assessment

Consider your own performance on the following "work habits."

- ◆ Wellness: Does this organization – your current employer – have specific guidelines and/or requirements for your wellness? Sleep requirements, body mass index, sobriety, certificates of fitness, continuing education, etc.
  - What are they? How are you doing personally when it comes to meeting these guidelines and requirements? Are you performing at 100%? If not, then what percentage would you give your performance? Where is the gap? What do you need to do to improve?
- ◆ Self-presentation: Does this organization – your current employer – have specific guidelines and/or requirements? Body mass index, height, hair length or style, dress code, uniform, etiquette, etc.
  - What are they? How are you doing personally when it comes to meeting these guidelines and requirements? Are you performing at 100%? If not, then what percentage would you give your performance? Where is the gap? What do you need to do to improve?
- ◆ Timeliness: Does this organization – your current employer – have specific guidelines and/or requirements? Shift schedules, arrival times, break times, departure times, and deadlines, and so on . . .
  - What are they? How are you doing personally when it comes to meeting these guidelines and requirements? Are you performing at 100%? If not, then what percentage would you give your performance? Where is the gap? What do you need to do to improve?
- ◆ Productivity: Does this organization – your current employer – have specific guidelines and/or requirements? Number of tasks completed per hour or per day, etc.
  - What are they? How are you doing personally when it comes to meeting these guidelines and requirements? Are you performing at 100%? If not, then what percentage would you give your performance? Where is the gap? What do you need to do to improve?

- ◆ Organization: Does this organization – your current employer – have specific guidelines and/or requirements? Specific systems for documenting and tracking tasks, responsibilities, and projects; note-taking, checklists, project plans, filing, etc.
  - What are they? How are you doing personally when it comes to meeting these guidelines and requirements? Are you performing at 100%? If not, then what percentage would you give your performance? Where is the gap? What do you need to do to improve?
- ◆ Attention to detail: Does this organization – your current employer – have specific guidelines and/or requirements? Standard operating procedures, quality assurance, double-checking, triple-checking, etc.
  - What are they? How are you doing personally when it comes to meeting these guidelines and requirements? Are you performing at 100%? If not, then what percentage would you give your performance? Where is the gap? What do you need to do to improve?
- ◆ Follow-through and consistency: Does this organization – your current employer – have specific guidelines and/or requirements? Maximum response times, etc.
  - What are they? How are you doing personally when it comes to meeting these guidelines and requirements? Are you performing at 100%? If not, then what percentage would you give your performance? Where is the gap? What do you need to do to improve?
- ◆ Initiative: Does this organization – your current employer – have specific guidelines and/or requirements? Are you identifying problems while they are still small and contributing to the solutions? Identifying and seizing opportunities without overstepping your bounds? Learning, sharing knowledge, taking action?
  - Are you clear about what it looks like to go the extra mile in your current role? Do you know how far you are permitted to go, when going above and beyond? How far is too far – overstepping? What can you do better?

Good Work Habits: Lesson Plan #3 – Self-Improvement Planning

Make a plan for improving your "work habits."

- Wellness: What are the requirements? What is your personal goal for improvement in the near future? What resources and support are available? What is your plan? What is your first step? When?
- Self-presentation: What are the requirements? What is your personal goal for improvement in the near future? What resources and support are available? What is your plan? What is your first step? When?
- Timeliness: What are the requirements? What is your personal goal for improvement in the near future? What resources and support are available? What is your plan? What is your first step? When?
- Productivity: What are the requirements? What is your personal goal for improvement in the near future? What resources and support are available? What is your plan? What is your first step? When?
- Organization: What are the requirements? What is your personal goal for improvement in the near future? What resources and support are available? What is your plan? What is your first step? When?
- Attention to detail: What are the requirements? What is your personal goal for improvement in the near future? What resources and support are available? What is your plan? What is your first step? When?
- Follow-through and consistency: What are the requirements? What is your personal goal for improvement in the near future? What resources and support are available? What is your plan? What is your first step? When?
- Initiative: What are the requirements? What is your personal goal for improvement in the near future? What resources and support are available? What is your plan? What is your first step? When?

Good Work Habits: Lesson Plan #4 – Wellness
Wellness: Maintaining a healthy body, mind, and spirit/mood.

◆ Are you taking good care of your mind? What are the main sources of input for your mind right now? How can you expose your mind to a greater variety of input?

◆ Are you taking good care of your body? When do you sleep? What do you eat and drink? How do you exercise? What bad habits do you need to break?

◆ Are you taking good care of your mood/spirit? How is your mood right now? How is your mood usually? What sources of strength – teachers, friends, family, music, prayer, meditation, exercise, game, hobby, art, etc. – can you tap more often that will lift your spirit/mood?

◆ What are your goals?

• For taking good care of your mind:

• For taking good care of your body:

• For taking good care of your spirit/mood/:

◆ What resources and support might be available?

◆ What is your plan?

◆ What is your first step? When?

Good Work Habits: Lesson Plan #5 – Planning a Wellness Initiative

There are many different approaches to employer-sponsored employee wellness programs, including a wide range of potential services and products. Following are some of the most common approaches (and some very uncommon) for you to consider.

- Education on wellness best practices, provided internally or externally. This can be achieved through newsletters, flyers, videos, websites, apps, or through classes and discussion groups. These efforts typically focus on the most significant controllable variables – diet, exercise, sleep, substance use (especially tobacco), and dealing with common stressors.
- Exercise programs, either offered on-site or reimbursement for those offered externally.
- Healthful eating programs, including nutritional information and healthful food choices in cafeterias and kitchens at work.
- Weight-loss programs, ranging from on-site support groups to employee competitions.
- Smoking cessation programs.
- Substance-abuse cessation programs.
- Stress reduction and management programs.
- Anti-bullying programs.
- Online (or telephone) health advisers /coaches.
- On-site health care services, ranging from periodic health risk screenings and flu shots and the like to full-scale on-site health care clinics complete with doctors, nurses, dentists, and more.
- Walking meetings and/or "stretching" meetings.
- Ergonomic workspace and furniture.
- Napping rooms, which can double as meditation rooms.
- Game rooms offering games ranging from old-fashioned "ping-pong" to the latest video games.
- Massage and other spa-like services.

Step One: Inventory your current resources.

- Find out what your organization currently offers or currently supports and determine whether there might be resources easily obtained to offer or support additional programs.

◆ Of course, some of what your organization supports will be obvious. You probably already know if there is a company cafeteria with a "healthy food" option every day or if there is an on-site gym, a lunchtime walking group, or an after-work yoga class.

◆ But there may be policies (and accompanying resources) that are less obvious:

For example, some organizations support wellness by offering discounts on health insurance premiums to those who participate in wellness programs or who meet certain benchmarks on key risk variables such as body mass, blood pressure, smoking, substance use, etc. Meanwhile, some employers impose penalties on employees who do not participate or who fail to meet certain benchmarks.

Do some research internally using the preceding list (and anything else you can think of) to see what your organization already offers or supports or might be willing to support. Ask your boss. Ask HR. Look online. Ask around.

Step Two: Choose a point of focus for your wellness initiative.

You could always make a decree as the manager and choose a point of focus for a wellness program for your team and see if they go along with it:

◆ From now on, one-on-one meetings will be walking meetings.
◆ Lunchtime or after work exercise group – running or yoga or whatever.
◆ Massage therapist will be coming around once a week.
◆ Weight loss competition: Who can lose the most weight?

But you will almost surely get much greater interest and more enthusiastic participation if they participate in choosing the focus. Bring the team together and have a group discussion. Sometimes there will be a strong consensus to focus on one thing or another. In a larger team, there may be small groups that coalesce around one focus or another.

Step Three: Remember that most of the meaningful efforts employees can make to improve their own wellness will have to be done on their own time at their own initiative.

Encourage employees to share their wellness goals up front and share their progress along the way. One thing you can do is provide recognition, credit, and possibly even rewards for those who meet specific wellness goals. (My advice is to talk to your boss or someone in HR and see what resources might be available and whether doing so would be in keeping with your organization's policies.)

Good Work Habits: Lesson Plan #6 – Self-Presentation

Self-presentation: Controlling your grooming, attire, and manners – given the social/cultural situation at hand – so as to make a positive impression on others.

◆ How would you describe your current approach to self-presentation?
  • Grooming:

  • Attire:

  • Manners:

◆ In this organization are there formal requirements or guidelines for self-presentation?
  • Grooming: Hair, cleanliness, etc.
  • Attire: Is there a uniform?
  • Manners: "Yes, sir. Yes, ma'am." Etc.

◆ In this organization are their formal requirements or guidelines for self-presentation?
  • Grooming: Hair, cleanliness, etc.
  • Attire: Is there a uniform?
  • Manners: "Yes, sir. Yes, ma'am." Etc.
◆ What about informally: In this organization are their informal guidelines that most people follow?
  • Grooming: Hair, cleanliness, etc.
  • Attire: Is there a uniform?
  • Manners: "Yes, sir. Yes, ma'am." Etc.
◆ What is the message being sent by the guidelines in this organization – whether they are formal or informal?
◆ Where do you fit – in relation to the informal or formal guidelines in this organization?
  • Grooming: Hair, cleanliness, etc.
  • Attire: Is there a uniform?
  • Manners: "Yes, sir. Yes, ma'am." Etc.

- What is the message that you want to send when it comes to your self-presentation?
- Where do you fit – in relation to the informal or formal guidelines in this organization? What message does that send?
  - Grooming: Hair, cleanliness, etc.
  - Attire: Is there a uniform?
  - Manners: "Yes, sir. Yes, ma'am." Etc.
- Is there anything you should change?

Good Work Habits: Lesson Plan #7 – Using a Time Log to Learn to Start Living by a Schedule

Learning to maintain an old-fashioned time log is a great way to begin to understand how you actually use your time inside and outside of work. The tool is very simple, but the insights can be profound when you see how you actually use that precious limited resource – your time.

Step One: Using the time log tool here, think back over the last 24 hours and try to reconstruct exactly how you used your time – hour by hour. Start with right now and work backward 24 hours or so, noting as best you can, hour by hour, what you were doing:

Today	Yesterday
12:01am	
1	
2	
3	
4	
5	
6	
7	
8	
9	
10	
11	
1	
2	
3	
4	
5	
6	
7	
8	
9	
10	
11	
11:59pm	

Step Two: Now look back over the past 24-hour time log you just completed. Is this a typical 24-hour period? If not, go back and make notes about where your typical day might differ from the last 24 hours.

Step Three: Now make a list of your top priorities in life and at work.

Step Four: Compare your list of top priorities with your time log for a typical 24-hour period. How does your time spending line up with your top priorities?

Step Five: Look at your own schedule.

STOP: Do you keep a schedule? Do you live by a schedule? If you do not already keep a schedule, take out your handheld device. You almost surely already have multiple scheduling apps, complete with automated reminders, from which you can choose. Choose one and make a note to familiarize yourself with it.

Write out your schedule for the coming 24 hours, hour by hour.

Today	Tomorrow
12:01am	
1	
2	
3	
4	
5	
6	
7	
8	
9	
10	
11	
1	
2	
3	
4	
5	

Today	Tomorrow
6	
7	
8	
9	
10	
11	
11:59pm	

Now take a look and ask yourself: How does that schedule for the next 24 hours line up with your top priorities? Are there any changes you need to make?

Step Six: Now consider your schedule for the coming week.

> STOP: If you are just familiarizing yourself with a scheduling app, this is the time to schedule some key appointments for the coming week:

- ◆ What time do you arrive for work each day? Plug in your arrival time for work each day.
- ◆ How much time do you need to get to work? Plug in a reminder to depart for work on time each day.
- ◆ How much time do you need to get ready for work before you depart? Plug in an alarm to start getting ready.
- ◆ Now fill in key appointments for the coming week.

Now take a look at your schedule for the coming week and ask yourself: How does your schedule line up with your top priorities? Are there any changes you need to make?

Step Seven: HOMEWORK. Keep a real-time time log for the next week. Do it hour by hour or in fifteen-minute increments. Every time you switch activities, take note. Do it for a whole week.

Step Eight: AFTER COMPLETING HOMEWORK: Evaluate your full-week real-time time log:

- Examine your time log to identify your biggest time wasters. What are your lowest priority activities that are taking up your time? How can you eliminate them?
- Examine your time log to identify your biggest sources of interruption. What can you do to better manage those interruptions?
- Examine your time log to identify any unexpected emergencies or urgent matters that required your attention. What can you do to better anticipate and prevent such matters going forward?
- Examine your time log to identify opportunities to increase your efficiency. What can you streamline? What shortcuts can you take? What detours can you avoid?
- Now make your schedule for the coming week, taking into account what you've learned from keeping the time log.

Step Nine: Repeat steps seven and eight for as many weeks in a row as you can stand.

Good Work Habits: Lesson Plan #8 – How to Make a Basic Project Plan

Step One: Choose your most important project on which to focus. What is the big goal? What is the deadline? What are the specifications?

Step Two: Working backward from the deadline, break that big goal into intermediate goals with intermediate deadlines:

Intermediate Goals	Intermediate Deadlines
-	
-	
-	
-	
-	
-	

Step Three: Working backward from each intermediate goal and deadline, break each intermediate goal and deadline into a timetable of concrete action steps.

Intermediate Goals	Intermediate Deadlines	Action Steps/Timetable
Intermediate goal	Intermediate deadline	
		1
		2
		3
		4
		5
Intermediate goal	Intermediate deadline	
		1
		2
		3
		4
		5

Intermediate Goals	Intermediate Deadlines	Action Steps/Timetable
Intermediate Goal	Intermediate Deadline	
		-1
		-2
		-3
		-4
		-5

Step Four: Now make a step-by-step plan going forward, with a time budget for each action step, from day one until the final deadline. Every day consult your step-by-step plan, and make a list of action steps, noting the time budget you have allowed, and any guidelines and specifications. That's how to bring a plan alive and put it into action: Use it every day to make your to-do list.

Step Five: Make sure to track your progress and make sure you are meeting your timetables for each concrete action step along the way to each intermediate deadline. Track your progress to make sure you are meeting each intermediate deadline. If you are off track, you need to revisit the plan, and revise and adjust your timetables . . . or else speed up!

Good Work Habits: Lesson Plan #9 – Taking Notes and Making Checklists

Step One: Make a list of your recurring tasks or responsibilities.

Step Two: Take it one task/responsibility at a time. Start with your number one task/responsibility. Brainstorm:

- What information do you need to return to regularly? How do you keep track of it? What can you do to take better notes?
- What information will you want to pass on to someone else? How do you keep track of it? What can you do to take better notes?
- What information will you need to return to at a specific time in the future? How do you keep track of it? What can you do to take better notes?

Now go through the rest of your tasks/responsibilities and brainstorm the preceding questions for each one.

Step Three: Brainstorm: What is your current system for taking notes and keeping track of information? How can you improve on your current system?

Step Four: Brainstorm: What information tools do you currently have available to you in order to help you keep track of that information? Do you currently use checklists to guide you? On which tasks/responsibilities would checklists be helpful tools to guide you?

Step Five: Make checklists to guide you on any recurring task or responsibility. Take it one task/responsibility at a time. All checklists really are is a list of very detailed step-by-step instructions:

- First, write out step-by-step instructions for the task, from memory. Break each task into its component steps, and break each step into a series of concrete actions.

- Second, perform the task, very slowly, keeping one eye on the step-by-step instructions you prepared. As you perform the task, make corrections and additions to your step-by-step instructions.

- Third, perform the task again, very slowly, and make further corrections and additions. Include as many details on each step – and in between each step – as you can think of. Make a checklist for each item within the checklist. Seriously: Take each step and break it down into smaller pieces so there is a mini-checklist for each item.

- Fourth, write a new draft of step-by-step instructions in the form of a checklist.

- Fifth, ask someone else to try using your checklist to guide them and see if it works for them. Get their suggestions for further corrections and additions.

- Sixth, going forward, use this checklist to guide you in completing your task and also for making notes along the way going forward. Remember the key is actually using the checklists. You have to "check" as you complete each item on the checklist. Make notes in the margins of the checklists as you use them.

Good Work Habits: Lesson Plan #10 – How to Do a Time/Motion Study on Your Own Work

Step One: Make a list of your recurring tasks or responsibilities. Take it one task/responsibility at a time. Start with your number one task/responsibility.

Step Two: For this task, if you have a checklist, use the checklist to help you do your time/motion study. You'll need to actually perform the task to do this time/motion study properly.

- One task at a time, do the task multiple times.
- If you don't already have a checklist, you'll have to break each task into its component steps; and break each step into a series of concrete actions.
- As you perform the task, time the whole task; time each step within each task, and time each concrete action within each step.
- How long does each task take? Each step within each task? Each concrete action within each step? How long should they take? Create a time budget for every concrete action – for every step – for every task.

That's a time/motion study.

Step Three: Take it to the next level by using your time/motion budgets to help you keep score for yourself going forward.

- If you are behind schedule, do a micro-gap analysis. Identify the micro-gaps between the time budget you made and your actual time step-by-step, concrete action by concrete action. In these micro-gaps lie the potential opportunities to speed up.
- If you want to speed up, choose one concrete action at a time to "accelerate" and take it slowly. Close the micro-gaps one by one. By going one concrete action at time, you will minimize the chances of increased mistakes in the effort to speed up.
- Are you sure you are doing each concrete step correctly?
- Are you doing any unnecessary actions or steps that might slow you down?
- Are you encountering any recurring obstacles that can be removed?

Good Work Habits: Lesson Plan #11 – Spotlight on Follow-Through

Step One: Brainstorm. What does it mean to you to "follow through" on your commitments at work? Why is follow-through important?

Step Two: Make a list of all of your current tasks, responsibilities, and projects. For each one, make note of the following: What is your next deliverable and when is it due? What was the last time you took action on it? What is the next step you need to take to move that task, responsibility, or project forward?

Tasks/Projects	Next Deliverable	Last Action Taken	Next Step

Step Three: What can you do to close out work that should not still be open?

Good Work Habits: Lesson Plan #12 – Going the Extra Mile

Step One: Brainstorm. What does it mean to you to "take initiative" at work? What does it mean to "go the extra mile"? What does it mean to go "above and beyond"?

Step Two: Make a list of all of your current tasks, responsibilities, and projects. What are all the aspects of doing your job very well, very fast, all day long?

Step Three: Now, next to each task, responsibility, and project, take note: What would it look like for you to go the extra mile on that task, responsibility, or project? After you do your job very well, very fast, all day long – in those extra moments – what are some extra ways you can add value?

Make an "extra mile" list for yourself: A list of all the extra ways you can go above and beyond on every task, responsibility, and project.

Step Four: HOMEWORK. Every single item on your extra mile list is a concrete opportunity to excel in your current role. How often do you complete items on your extra mile list? Keep score for yourself going forward.

Teaching Interpersonal Communication Skills

Interpersonal communication: Attentive listening, observing, and reading; perceiving and empathizing; effective and appropriate use of words, tone, expressions, and gestures – verbal, written, and otherwise; one-on-one and in groups; in-person and remotely.

BRIDGING THE GAP

Are more and more people today becoming weaker at interpersonal communication simply because we are all becoming so accustomed to communicating with our devices and losing the ability to communicate well in person and on the phone?

That's surely a big part of the story. Communication practices are habits and most of us are more and more in the habit of remote informal staccato and relatively low-stakes interpersonal communication because of our constant use of handheld devices and the mores of social media and instant messaging.

The crux of people skills is "other orientation," paying close attention to the signals of those with whom you are interacting, without getting distracted, and then responding to those signals effectively and appropriately. But people today, isolated as so many of us are, become very self-focused. Plus, we are perpetually distracted. As we become less accustomed to engaging in person, perhaps our powers of interpersonal perception are diminishing.

Think of it this way. Have you ever had a big misunderstanding (or fight) with someone via text messaging? Often that happens partly because words alone, especially informal staccato messages, are very easy to misunderstand. That's because tone, expressions, and gestures are a very big part of how human beings communicate. So much meaning is lost or misconstrued in texts. Now throw in the social media dimension – in which communication is an interactive performance among peers (or not even peers, but the virtual personas of peers). This is the information environment in which more and more of us are honing our interpersonal communication practices. Even many in-person interactions are increasingly underwritten and mediated by social media network relationships.

There is structure in most workplaces. Nonetheless a shocking amount of the important communication in most workplaces is largely ad hoc, hit and miss. There is a lot of "touching base" or "call me if you need me," mediocre meetings, and long multi-recipient email chains, but there is usually way too little regular structured communication. No wonder most people don't realize that the burden is on them to ensure their interpersonal communication at work is more structured and substantive.

Like any other habits, communication habits can be changed, but it is not easy.

Putting more structure and substance into your communication – regular, structured, one-on-one dialogues – will give you the chance to practice interacting in a more professional manner. Over time, learn to prepare better and better agendas for your one-on-ones, to make them increasingly organized, clear, and focused.

Here's why you should care about improving your people skills. Even though it seems like your interactions with other people are a matter of personal style, in fact there are proven best practices for workplace communication. When people do not follow communication best practices, things are much more likely to go wrong. Poor communication is the number one cause of unnecessary problems – great and small – in the workplace.

Poor communication also leads to suboptimal workplace relationships, including conflicts between and among employees.

No matter where you work or what you do, good interpersonal communication skills will help you get ahead faster. Poor interpersonal communication skills will always hold you back. Some people are known as being really great to work with, while others are known for being difficult. In either case, that's almost always a commentary on the person's communication practices. You want to be known as someone who is great to work with.

That means you need to learn best practices and build new habits to:

◆ Learn how to tune in to other people and read them more effectively;
◆ Take on the burden of putting more structure and substance into your communication with key people; and
◆ Learn best practices for expressing yourself more effectively – one-on-one and in groups – in person and remotely.

If you learn those best practices and develop better habits, you will avoid many more unnecessary problems, you will build much better workplace relationships, and you will gain a reputation as one of those people with whom others want to work.

Interpersonal Communication Skills: Lesson Plan #1 – Introduction

Self-assessment. Consider your own personal track record when it comes to the following "interpersonal communication" best practices.

- Listen twice as much as you talk.
  Give yourself a grade (+A-, +B-, +C-, +D-, F). How can you improve?

- Never interrupt or let your mind wander when others are speaking.
  Give yourself a grade (+A-, +B-, +C-, +D-, F). How can you improve?

- Empathize. Always try to imagine yourself in the other person's position.
  Give yourself a grade (+A-, +B-, +C-, +D-, F). How can you improve?

- Exhibit respect, kindness, courtesy, and good manners.
  Give yourself a grade (+A-, +B-, +C-, +D-, F). How can you improve?

- Prepare in advance before meetings or one-on-one conversations so you are brief, direct, and clear.
  Give yourself a grade (+A-, +B-, +C-, +D-, F). How can you improve?

- Never speak of a problem unless you have thought of at least one potential solution.
  Give yourself a grade (+A-, +B-, +C-, +D-, F). How can you improve?

- Take personal responsibility for everything you say and do.
  Give yourself a grade (+A-, +B-, +C-, +D-, F). How can you improve?

- Don't make excuses when you make a mistake.
  Give yourself a grade (+A-, +B-, +C-, +D-, F). How can you improve?

- Don't blame or complain.
  Give yourself a grade (+A-, +B-, +C-, +D-, F). How can you improve?

- Don't take yourself too seriously.
  Give yourself a grade (+A-, +B-, +C-, +D-, F). How can you improve?

- Always take your commitments and responsibilities seriously.
  Give yourself a grade (+A-, +B-, +C-, +D-, F). How can you improve?

- Always give people credit for their achievements, no matter how small.
  Give yourself a grade (+A-, +B-, +C-, +D-, F). How can you improve?

Interpersonal Communication Skills: Lesson Plan #2 – Self-Assessment

Consider the following "interpersonal communication" best practices and what they mean to you.

- ◆ Listen twice as much as you talk.

  What are the business reasons for this best practice? What are the reasons why it is in your best interests as an employee to follow this best practice? Are there good reasons to NOT follow this best practice?

- ◆ Never interrupt or let your mind wander when others are speaking.

  What are the business reasons for this best practice? What are the reasons why it is in your best interests as an employee to follow this best practice? Are there good reasons to NOT follow this best practice?

- ◆ Empathize. Always try to imagine yourself in the other person's position.

  What are the business reasons for this best practice? What are the reasons why it is in your best interests as an employee to follow this best practice? Are there good reasons to NOT follow this best practice?

- ◆ Exhibit respect, kindness, courtesy, and good manners.

  What are the business reasons for this best practice? What are the reasons why it is in your best interests as an employee to follow this best practice? Are there good reasons to NOT follow this best practice?

- ◆ Prepare in advance before meetings or one-on-one conversations so you are brief, direct, and clear.

  What are the business reasons for this best practice? What are the reasons why it is in your best interests as an employee to follow this best practice? Are there good reasons to NOT follow this best practice?

- ◆ Never speak of a problem unless you have thought of at least one potential solution.

What are the business reasons for this best practice? What are the reasons why it is in your best interests as an employee to follow this best practice? Are there good reasons to NOT follow this best practice?

♦ Take personal responsibility for everything you say and do.
What are the business reasons for this best practice? What are the reasons why it is in your best interests as an employee to follow this best practice? Are there good reasons to NOT follow this best practice?

♦ Don't make excuses when you make a mistake.
What are the business reasons for this best practice? What are the reasons why it is in your best interests as an employee to follow this best practice? Are there good reasons to NOT follow this best practice?

♦ Don't blame or complain.
What are the business reasons for this best practice? What are the reasons why it is in your best interests as an employee to follow this best practice? Are there good reasons to NOT follow this best practice?

♦ Don't take yourself too seriously.
What are the business reasons for this best practice? What are the reasons why it is in your best interests as an employee to follow this best practice? Are there good reasons to NOT follow this best practice?

♦ Always take your commitments and responsibilities seriously.
What are the business reasons for this best practice? What are the reasons why it is in your best interests as an employee to follow this best practice? Are there good reasons to NOT follow this best practice?

♦ Always give people credit for their achievements, no matter how small.
What are the business reasons for this best practice? What are the reasons why it is in your best interests as an employee to follow this best practice? Are there good reasons to NOT follow this best practice?

Interpersonal Communication Skills: Lesson Plan #3 – Learning to Use the "People List"

Learn to make a people list.

Step One: Make a list of all the key people you interact with at work on a regular basis and put them into the following categories:

- ◆ Leaders, managers, and supervisors to whom you report directly or indirectly
- ◆ Coworkers on your team
- ◆ Coworkers outside your team
- ◆ Anyone who directly reports to you as their manager
- ◆ Outside partners or vendors

Step Two: Now take them one person at a time. For each person on your list in step one, answer the following questions:

- ◆ WHO?

  Who is this person at work? What role does this person play in relation to you and your job? Is this person highly regarded by others, as far as you know? Do you hold this person in high regard?

- ◆ WHY?

  What is your primary reason for interacting with this person at work? What are the circumstances that cause you to interact with this person? What are the conditions? What are you trying to accomplish in your interactions with this person? What are your goals for your interactions with this person?

- ◆ WHAT?

  What is the substance of the communication you need to have with this person? What do you need to learn from this communication? What does the other person need from you? What information exchange do you need to accomplish? What are the right words?

- ◆ HOW?

  How do you usually interact with this person? Do you ask questions? Or do you give instructions? Do you spell things out in detail? Or are you specific or vague? Are you direct or indirect? How do you think this person would prefer you interact?

♦ WHERE?

If you meet in person, then where do you meet usually? If you do not meet in person, then where do the conversations take place: By telephone? Email? Text? Or otherwise? One-on-one? In meetings? Where do you think this person would prefer to interact?

♦ WHEN?

When do you usually interact with this person? What days and times typically? And how often? When do you think this person would prefer to interact with you?

This is a great tool to help you tune in better to any person with whom you need to interact on a regular basis. You can use this tool any time you want to try to better understand where a person is coming from and how to be more effective in your communication practices with this person.

Step Three: Take this exercise to the next level by turning these six questions into a powerful tool for staying tuned in to other people at work and maintaining better interpersonal communication.

Arrange the six questions (just the shorthand) along the top of a page in a horizontal axis, either on paper or in a simple spreadsheet. In the "WHO" column, write the names of all the key people with whom you interact. Then make some notes in answer to the question: "Who is this person in relation to you at work?" Then for each person, answer the other five questions and make some notes in each column alongside that person's name in the same horizontal row. Answer all the questions for everybody on your list. That's how you make a "people list."

Who	Why	What	How	Where	When

Step Four: After you've made your first people list, it shouldn't be your last. HOMEWORK: Try making a people list at least once a week. Do it at the beginning of each week. Set up the columns. Then make a list of the key people with whom you need to interact that week: leaders, coworkers, direct reports, and anyone else. Go through and make some notes in answer to each of the six questions for each person. That's a great way to set yourself up for success in your interpersonal communication that week!

Step Five: Take this exercise even further by using a slightly different version of this tool to interview the key people with whom you interact and ask them directly how they would like you to structure your interpersonal communication with them going forward.

◆ WHO?

How would you describe the role you play here? From your perspective, where do I fit in relation to you?

◆ WHY?

From your perspective, what is the primary reason we interact? What do you need to accomplish when interacting with me? What should my goals be when I am interacting with you?

◆ WHAT?

What is the substance of the communication we need to have? What should I be trying to learn from this communication? What do you need to learn from me? What information do you need from me? What are the right words for me to say to you?

◆ HOW?

How would you prefer we interact? Would you prefer that I ask questions or just answer questions? Do you want to give me instructions or do you need instructions from me? Do you need things in detail or just the big picture?

◆ WHERE?

Does meeting in person work better for you? If so, where would you prefer to meet? If meeting in person is not an option, then where do you prefer the conversations take place: By telephone? Email? Text? Or otherwise? One-on-one? In meetings?

◆ WHEN?

What days and times work best for you? How often do you think we need to meet?

Consider taking the time to interview all the key people with whom you interact. Use the interview as a learning process and as an opportunity to plan together with each person for how you will communicate going forward.

Interpersonal Communication Skills: Lesson Plan #4 – Put More Structure into Your Communication

Put more structure into your communication.

Step One: High structure means regularly scheduled and conducted according to a clear, well-organized agenda with lots of give-and-take.

Brainstorming Questions: How many of your important conversations at work are high structure by this definition? Which ones are high structure? Which ones are low structure? Why?

Step Two: What can you do to put more structure into more of your important conversations?

- ◆ Can you schedule them? Which ones? When?
- ◆ Can you create a clear, well-organized agenda? For which ones?
- ◆ What can you do to put more give-and-take into your conversations? Are you usually giving or taking? Can you adjust the balance?

Step Three: Look at your schedule, or consider your typical day or week. How much time can you set aside each day for regular structured communication? Can you block out time every day? Every other day? Twice a week? How many scheduled one-on-one conversations can you fit into that time you blocked out in step three?

Step Four: Make a list of the key people with whom you need to interact: your managers, coworkers inside and outside your team, your direct reports, and anyone else. Start with the most important conversations and schedule as many one-on-one conversations as you can squeeze in.

Step Five: Consider the following best practices.

- ◆ Is it possible to choose a regular time, and stick with it as long as you can? If you have to make a change, try to set a new regular time, and try to stick with the new time as long as you can.

◆ Is it possible to have in-person meetings? If you have to meet remotely, don't let the phone call slip. And make sure to support these telephone conversations with clear point-by-point e-mails before and after your calls. Follow-up e-mails are key, especially following telephone one-on-ones.

◆ Is it possible to meet in the same place? Choose a good venue, whether it is your office, a conference room, or the stairwell. You want these meetings to become familiar and comfortable. The routine of meeting in the same place every time is an important part of the structure these one-on-one meetings provide.

Interpersonal Communication Skills: Lesson Plan #5 – Put More Substance into Your Communication

Put more substance into your communication.

Step One: High substance means rich in relevant information.

Brainstorming Questions: How many of your important conversations at work are high substance by this definition? Which ones are high substance? Which ones are low substance? Why? What's the difference?

Step Two: Look at your schedule, or consider your typical day or week.

Make a list of the key people with whom you need to interact – your managers, coworkers inside and outside your team, your direct reports, and anyone else.

Make a list of conversations you anticipate having in the next week.

Step Three: Review your list of conversations you anticipate having and schedule as many of these conversations as possible.

Step Four: Choose one of the anticipated conversations to zero in on. Ask yourself what you can do to better prepare for the conversation:

- ◆ What can you do to prepare in advance?
- ◆ Do you have a clear agenda for the meeting?
- ◆ What information do you need to deliver, and in what form?
- ◆ Is there a document you can prepare in advance to make it more clear?
- ◆ What key points will you want to address verbally? Make a list of those key points.
- ◆ What information do you need to capture and in what form?
- ◆ Is there an information capture tool you can prepare in advance to make it easier?
- ◆ What key questions will you want to ask? Make a list of key questions.

Are there some parts of the conversation that might be difficult? If so, you should consider writing a script and even rehearsing it before the conversation. (You don't have to stick exactly to the script, but it might help you if you get nervous or thrown off during the actual conversation.)

What can you do to put more give-and-take into your conversations? Are you usually giving or taking? Can you adjust the balance?

Be prepared to wrap up each conversation with the following questions:

◆ Exactly what is my next deliverable on this? To whom? By what deadline?

◆ What guidelines and specifications should I follow?

◆ Do you want me to prepare a short step-by-step plan first and run it by you?

◆ When should we talk next? Let's schedule our next conversation now: When? Where? What will be our agenda?

Step Five: HOMEWORK. Use this tool going forward to prepare in advance for conversations. Modify it any way you like to make it more useful.

Interpersonal Communication Skills: Lesson Plan #6 – Preparing for Meetings

Consider the following best practices for preparing for meetings.

- Before attending any meeting or presentation, make sure you know what the meeting is about and whether your attendance is required or requested.
  Give yourself a grade (+A-, +B-, +C-, +D-, F). How can you improve?

- Identify what your role in the meeting is. What information are you responsible for communicating or gathering? Prepare in advance: Is there any material you should review or read before the meeting? Are there any conversations you need to have before the meeting?
  Give yourself a grade (+A-, +B-, +C-, +D-, F). How can you improve?

- If you are making a presentation, prepare even more. Ask yourself exactly what value you have to offer the group.
  Give yourself a grade (+A-, +B-, +C-, +D-, F). How can you improve?

- If you are not a primary actor in the meeting, often the best thing you can do is say as little as possible and practice good meeting manners: Do not multitask, make unnecessary noise or activity; stay focused on the business at hand.
  Give yourself a grade (+A-, +B-, +C-, +D-, F). How can you improve?

- If you are tempted to speak up, ask yourself: Is this a point that everyone needs to hear, right here and now? If you have a question, could it be asked at a later time?
  Give yourself a grade (+A-, +B-, +C-, +D-, F). How can you improve?

- If you don't have a clear role in the meeting and yet find yourself there anyway, try not to say a single word that will unnecessarily lengthen it.
  Give yourself a grade (+A-, +B-, +C-, +D-, F). How can you improve?

Interpersonal Communication Skills: Lesson Plan #7 – Email Best Practices

Consider the following best practices for email communication.

- Send fewer and better messages.
  Give yourself a grade (+A-, +B-, +C-, +D-, F). How can you improve?

- Before sending a message, always ask yourself if this is really something that should be communicated in person at a scheduled one-on-one or a scheduled meeting.
  Give yourself a grade (+A-, +B-, +C-, +D-, F). How can you improve?

- Stop sending first drafts! Send first drafts to yourself.
  Give yourself a grade (+A-, +B-, +C-, +D-, F). How can you improve?

- If you are messaging so you don't forget, then send the reminder to yourself!
  Give yourself a grade (+A-, +B-, +C-, +D-, F). How can you improve?

- Only cc people who need to be cc'd.
  Give yourself a grade (+A-, +B-, +C-, +D-, F). How can you improve?

- Use red flags and other indicators sparingly and with true purpose.
  Give yourself a grade (+A-, +B-, +C-, +D-, F). How can you improve?

- Make subject lines smart; context is everything.
  Give yourself a grade (+A-, +B-, +C-, +D-, F). How can you improve?

- Change subject lines on later emails if the subject changes.
  Give yourself a grade (+A-, +B-, +C-, +D-, F). How can you improve?

- Make messages brief, simple, and orderly.
  Give yourself a grade (+A-, +B-, +C-, +D-, F). How can you improve?

◆ Create a simple folder system for filing incoming and outgoing electronic communication based on how YOU will use them later

Give yourself a grade (+A-, +B-, +C-, +D-, F). How can you improve?

◆ Establish time blocks daily when you will review and respond to electronic communication and let people know when to expect your responses

Give yourself a grade (+A-, +B-, +C-, +D-, F). How can you improve?

Interpersonal Communication Skills: Lesson Plan #8 – Communicating Remotely

Consider the following best practices for remote communication.

- ◆ Schedule group meetings only for good reasons: to create a feeling of belonging and cohesion, to communicate a bunch of information to everybody in the same way at the same time, to brainstorm, or to plan interdependent work. Make sure everyone who is invited knows exactly why they are needed at the meeting and exactly how they are expected to prepare in advance and participate.
  Give yourself a grade (+A-, +B-, +C-, +D-, F). How can you improve?

- ◆ Schedule regular (daily, weekly, at least every other week) one-on-ones with all of your key colleagues: Your boss, every one of your direct reports, and your key lateral colleagues.
  Give yourself a grade (+A-, +B-, +C-, +D-, F). How can you improve?

- ◆ Always prepare in advance in writing for remote meetings – one-on-one and group meetings. A written recap of where your last meeting left off and key issues since your last meeting: Updates? Decisions to be made? Resources? Troubleshooting? Information to be shared? Questions to be asked? Planning?
  Give yourself a grade (+A-, +B-, +C-, +D-, F). How can you improve?

- ◆ Share your written preparation in advance always before one-on-ones.
  Give yourself a grade (+A-, +B-, +C-, +D-, F). How can you improve?

- ◆ Always prepare and share and follow a clear agenda in writing before any group meeting if you are in charge.
  Give yourself a grade (+A-, +B-, +C-, +D-, F). How can you improve?

◆ Conduct some, but not all, of your remote meetings with video. For video meetings, turn cameras on.
    Give yourself a grade (+A-, +B-, +C-, +D-, F). How can you improve?

◆ Take good notes during all meetings and share a recap of your notes with key players afterward. If you can, recap what each person agreed to, and focus on the actions you specifically are committing to take, the steps you will follow, and the timeline; as well as the date and time of your next scheduled phone call; and then of course, prepare in advance and send any documents for review prior to the next meeting.
    Give yourself a grade (+A-, +B-, +C-, +D-, F). How can you improve?

Chapter 5

Teaching the Missing Basics of Critical Thinking

C ritical Thinking: The Missing Basics

- *Proactive learning*: Keeping an open mind, suspending judgment, questioning assumptions, and seeking out information, technique, and perspective; and studying, practicing, and contemplating in order to build your stored knowledge base, skillset, and wisdom.
- *Problem solving*: Mastering established best practices – proven, repeatable solutions for dealing with regular recurring decisions – so as to avoid reinventing the wheel. Using repeatable solutions to improvise when addressing decisions that are new but similar.
- *Decision making*: Information analysis, weighing competing arguments, extrapolation, and the ability to see the connections between cause and effect, to predict accurately the consequences of one choice as opposed to another.

Teaching Proactive Learning

Proactive learning: Keeping an open mind, suspending judgment, questioning assumptions, and seeking out information, technique, and perspective; and studying, practicing, and contemplating in order to build your stored knowledge base, skillset, and wisdom.

BRIDGING THE GAP

Before any individual can possibly succeed at "critical thinking," that person has to know some things. That way they will have

147

something – anything really – about which to think critically. Step one: Know something! Or know how to do something! Or have an appreciation for multiple competing perspectives about something.

It is almost a hackneyed truth about today's world that we all have endless amounts of information at our fingertips available instantly all the time. Indeed, we have multiple competing answers to any question on any subject – more answers than a whole platoon could possibly master in a lifetime on any subject. It is nearly as hackneyed to say that today's new young workforce has never known it any other way. The not quite as obvious punchline is this: There has been a radical change in the prevailing mindset how much information a person needs to keep inside the head versus accessible through the fingertips. Nobody should be so shortsighted or so old-fashioned as to write off the power of being able to find multiple competing answers to any question about any subject any time instantly. Yet this phenomenon is also at the root of the critical thinking skills gap.

Critical thinking is very difficult. It requires strong thinking muscles. Like any muscles, thinking muscles don't get strong overnight. If you're not in shape, you start by taking walks, not distance runs. If you've never lifted weights, you have to start off with lighter weights and work yourself up to the heavier lifting.

Critical thinking is also a very sophisticated skillset. It requires mental flexibility and agility. But if you try to stretch too much too fast without good form and good structural support, you are liable to pull a muscle. When it comes to critical thinking, stupid decisions are the equivalent of pulled muscles.

What is the best way to "build strong thinking muscles"? Exercise them regularly. That means studying information, practicing technique, and contemplating multiple competing perspectives.

What is the necessary "structural support"? Stored knowledge, skills, and wisdom:

- ◆ Stored knowledge is the result of studying good information.
- ◆ Stored skills are the result of practicing good technique.
- ◆ Stored wisdom is the result of contemplating multiple competing good perspectives.

What is "good form"? Keeping an open mind. That means suspending judgment, questioning assumptions, and continually seeking out the best new information, technique, and perspective.

That's why proactive learning is the first of the missing basics of critical thinking.

Here's why you should care about proactive learning. Of course, the more you learn, the more you will know. But there is more to it than that. All the leading research shows that the very act of learning also strengthens your mind. If you are not actively learning, then your mind is getting weaker – just like any underused muscle. No matter how smart you are, if you are not actively learning, then you are actually getting a little dumber every day. You probably won't notice. However, all the leading research says this is the case.

Even if you don't learn anything, the very act of trying to learn is great exercise for your brain. Your mind needs regular exercise to stay in shape and get stronger.

Critical thinking skills are incredibly valuable – among the most in-demand skills in nearly every sector of the labor market. The reason they are so valuable and in-demand is because they are considered to be in relatively short supply. That's because critical thinking is a whole lot harder than it looks. Critical thinkers do not leap to conclusions – they take the time to consider various possibilities and do not become too attached to one point of view. They do not latch onto one solution – they know that most solutions are temporary and improve over time with new data. They are in the habit of trying to differentiate between reliable and unreliable sources. They carefully weigh the strengths of conflicting views and apply logical reasoning. Critical thinkers are at once open to the views of others and supremely independent in their own judgments.

Think of the very smartest people you know. You can take this to the bank: They are probably also the most voracious learners you know. The biggest mistake that keeps a person from getting smarter is thinking that being smart is a fixed status, rather than a dynamic process. The smartest people are the ones who never declare victory over learning.

Yes, if you are a proactive learner, you will actually know more and more. But, as soon as you take what you already know – about anything whatsoever – and declare victory, you will be on the path to getting a little bit dumber – and not just about that specific matter. That means letting go of the idea that "being smart" means you already know everything.

That's why "proactive learning" is the first key building block for developing critical thinking skills. If you want to be really smart, act like you don't know anything and go from there. That's the first step to proactive learning: Keep an open mind. Then you will have lots of space to store a regular stream of new information, technique, and perspective. Study information and you will build your stored knowledge base. Practice technique and you will build your stored skill base. Contemplate different perspectives and you will build stored wisdom. Never declare victory. Keep learning.

No matter how smart you are, if you are in the habit of critical proactive learning, you will keep getting smarter. That's what makes proactive learning the ultimate transferable skill. And unlike the hot technical skills, it will never become obsolete.

Proactive Learning: Lesson Plan #1 – Knowledge Work

Step One: Consider the following statement: "Proactive learning is the first key to become a critical thinker."

Brainstorming questions: What does "proactive learning" mean to you? Can you think of specific examples? Why is proactive learning important? Why is it in the best interests of this organization – your current employer – to have employees who are committed to proactive learning? Why is it in your best interests as an employee to be committed to proactive learning? Are there downsides or good reasons to NOT be committed to proactive learning?

Step Two: Make a list of the subjects or areas inside or outside of work where you do the most proactive learning. What have you learned? How did you learn it? What did you actually do, step-by-step, in doing that proactive learning? Are you still in learning mode? What are you learning? How? What are you actually doing, step-by-step?

Step Three: Knowledge work is NOT about what you do, but rather, it is about HOW you do whatever you do. Any task, responsibility, or project is knowledge work if you leverage skill, knowledge, and wisdom in accomplishing it. Consider the following paragraph:

> FOR EXAMPLE: Even if you are digging a ditch, there is skill, knowledge, and wisdom you can leverage. What is the best way to grip the shovel? What is the most effective technique for striking the ground? What is the most effective technique for lifting the dirt? What kind of shovel should you use? What kind of gloves? What is the best physical posture? What is the best pace?

BRAINSTORM: Take a moment to clarify for yourself the precise meaning of skill, knowledge, and wisdom.

Skill (the mastery of technique). List examples:

Knowledge (the master of information). List examples:

Wisdom (the understanding of many, many perspectives). List examples:

Step Four: Now make a list of your tasks, responsibilities, and projects at work.

Take them one at a time. For each, ask yourself: Do some of them seem more to you like knowledge work, while other seem less like knowledge work? Which ones seem like knowledge work? Why? Which ones don't? Why?

Again, take them one at a time. For each, now consider: In doing this task, responsibility, or project, what can you do to leverage more skill, knowledge, and wisdom in order to do a better job? From what source could you gain that learning?

Step Five: At work, think of something about which you are really excited to learn more. Choose one of your tasks/responsibilities/projects from step four for which you could really benefit from doing some proactive learning. Now make a proactive learning plan.

LEARNING PLAN
First, spell out your learning goals and assess your available resources.

- ◆ Make a list of knowledge you want to master. What information do you need? From what sources? What resources are available

- ◆ Make a list of skills you want to master. What techniques do you need? From what sources? What resources are available?

♦ Make a list of the wisdom you wish to acquire. What perspectives do you need? From what sources? What resources are available?

Second, set concrete goals for yourself with a reasonable deadline and any guidelines or specifications.

Goals	Deadlines	Guidelines/Specifications

Third, for each goal, spell out a list of intermediate goals and deadlines.

Intermediate Goals/Deadlines Then, for each intermediate goal/deadline, spell out your concrete learning actions. For example:

♦ Research: Seek out information, technique, and/or perspective.
♦ Vet sources: Compare different sources and try to choose the best sources.
♦ Organize: Organize the raw information, technique, and perspective.
♦ Learn: Study the information until it turns into stored knowledge; or practice the techniques until they turn into stored skills; or contemplate the perspectives until they turn into stored wisdom.

Step Six: HOMEWORK OPTION. Go ahead and execute that learning plan!

Proactive Learning: Lesson Plan #2 – Open Mind

Step One: Consider the following statement: "Keeping an open mind is the first key to proactive learning."

Brainstorming questions: What does "keeping an open mind" mean to you? Can you think of specific examples? Why is keeping an open mind important to proactive learning?

Step Two: Consider the following: Let's assume closed-mindedness is the opposite of open-mindedness.

Brainstorming questions: What does "closed-mindedness" mean to you? Can you think of specific examples? Why does closed-mindedness get in the way of proactive learning?

Step Three: Make a list of at least 10 statements about which you are absolutely certain.

Step Four: Now take them one at a time. For each one, ask yourself:

- Why are you so sure?
- What assumptions are you making that have not been proven?
- What do you really know about this matter?
- What is your source of information?
- How much have you really investigated?
- What would it take for you to second-guess this statement?
- What would it take to change your mind?
- What would it take to prove you wrong about this?
- What if the opposite is true? What else must be true in order for this "opposite" to be true? Construct the strongest argument you can to prove the "opposite" statement:
  - What facts would be necessary?
  - What are the best reasons to consider the "opposite" statement?
  - What are the best reasons to believe the "opposite" statement?

Step Five: HOMEWORK OPTION. Choose at least one of the "opposite" statements from step four to research and prove true. Start with the list of "facts" that would be necessary for the "opposite" statement to be true. For each of those facts, ask yourself:

- What sources of information could confirm those facts?
- How can I access those sources of information?
- Where should I begin?

Frame your research inquiry, fact by fact:

What Sources?	Steps to Access Each Source	Start Here
FACTS		

Once you've done your research, write out an argument to prove your case. The key to framing a good argument is making very good use of the word "because."

FRAMEWORK FOR MAKING A GOOD ARGUMENT
Assertion/conclusion:

. . .is true *because*. . .
Fact/source, which is important because. . .
. . .if this fact is true, these other facts cannot be true. . .
OR
. . .if this fact is true, these other facts must also be true. . .

+

Fact/source, which is important because. . .
. . .if this fact is true, these other facts cannot be true. . .
OR
. . .if this fact is true, these other facts must also be true. . .

+

Fact/source, which is important because. . .
. . .if this fact is true, these other facts cannot be true. . .
OR
. . .if this fact is true, these other facts must also be true. . .

The more facts and sources, of course, the stronger the argument.

Proactive Learning: Lesson Plan #3 – Suspend Judgment, Question Assumptions, and Seek to Learn

Step One: Consider the following statement: "Keeping an open mind" means suspending judgment, questioning assumptions, and seeking to learn.

Brainstorming questions:

◆ What does "suspending judgment" mean to you? Can you think of specific examples? Why is "suspending judgment" an important part of keeping an open mind?

◆ What does "questioning assumptions" mean to you? Can you think of specific examples? Why is "questioning assumptions" an important part of keeping an open mind?

◆ What does "seeking to learn" mean to you? Can you think of specific examples? Why is "seeking to learn" an important part of keeping an open mind?

Step Two: Make a list of your current tasks, responsibilities, and projects at work.

Step Three: Take your tasks, responsibilities, and projects, one by one. For each one, consider this question: When performing this task, responsibility, or project, what are the key moments when it would be really helpful to keep an open mind?

Step Four: For each of those key moments, try using the mantra of "open mindedness":

◆ Suspend judgment
◆ Question assumptions
◆ Seek to learn

For each, ask yourself:

Do I have a clear picture in my head? What parts of the picture seem the most clear? Are those clear parts of the picture in fact untested assumptions? How can I test those assumptions?

Interrogate every single assumption. How do I know that? What is my source of information? Is that a reliable source? Is there another source? Does it fit with common sense? Does it fit with everything else I know? Am I sure? How sure am I? The reason to question assumptions is to figure out what you don't know for sure so you can be clear about what you need to learn.

Proactive Learning: Lesson Plan #4 – Question Assumptions: What Do You Know? What Don't You Know?

Step One: Make a list of your current tasks, responsibilities, and projects at work.

Step Two: Take your tasks, responsibilities, and projects, one by one. For each one, ask yourself:

- What do you know about this task, responsibility, or project? Make a list of everything you know about it and how you know what you know. What assumptions are you making? What can you do to check your assumptions? What else can you learn?
- What don't you know about this task, responsibility, or project? Make a list of everything you don't know and what sources of information might hold the answers. What can you do to start tapping those sources and filling in those gaps in your knowledge?

Step Three: HOMEWORK OPTION. Choose one of your tasks, responsibilities, or projects from your list in step two – choose one about which you want to do some proactive learning.

- Start with your list of everything you think you know and double-check every single fact. See what you find.
- Now take the list of everything you do not know and your preliminary list of sources. One by one, source by source, go get the answers.
- Pay close attention to what you learn!

Proactive Learning: Lesson Plan #5 – Seeking Out Information, Technique, and Perspective

Step One: Research may be defined as "identifying and defining information needs so as to ask the right questions and then gathering good information from reliable sources quickly to get accurate and useful answers to those questions." What experiences have you had conducting research (at work, in school, or in your personal life)? When have you conducted research on a subject? What subject? What steps did you follow? What did you learn? What did you learn from that experience about the process of research itself? If you had to design a research project now on another topic, what steps would you follow?

Step Two: Remember the distinction between knowledge, skill, and wisdom:

- ◆ Knowledge comes from studying good information.
- ◆ Skill comes from practicing good technique.
- ◆ Wisdom comes from appreciating and understanding multiple perspectives.

Brainstorm: What different research tactics might one use for researching "information" to build knowledge, versus "technique" to build skill, versus "perspective" to build wisdom? What different sources might one use for researching "information" versus "technique" versus "wisdom"?

Step Three: Consider this: The first key to research is asking good questions:

Brainstorm: Consider the following elements of a good research question:

- ◆ Relevant to something that is of interest or concern
- ◆ Open-ended but not too open
- ◆ Focused but not too closed

- Narrow enough in scope that it can be answered in the time available
- Clear
- Evident questions: who, where, when
- Less evident questions: why, how, what

Brainstorm: What other elements might be important to a good research question?

Brainstorm: How might your research questions differ when it comes to "information" versus "technique" versus "perspective"?

Step Four: Consider this: The second key to research is finding good sources to answer your research questions:

Brainstorm: Consider the following elements of a good source:

- Proven expertise based on experience, education, or research.
- Validated and recognized by independent third parties.
- Facts are clearly distinguished from opinions.
- Facts are not merely asserted, but include explanations for how they were determined.
- Facts make sense in terms of other demonstrable facts.
- When facts diverge from other demonstrable facts, and that is acknowledged and explained.
- Alternative facts and arguments are acknowledged and explained.

Brainstorm: What other elements might be important in a good source?

Brainstorm: How might your best sources differ when it comes to "information" versus "technique" versus "perspective"?

Step Five: Make a list of your current tasks, responsibilities, and projects at work. Now choose one for which you would benefit from doing some research. Choose one about which you would be excited to do some research. Make a research plan:

The first key: Write your research questions.

What is the primary, overall question you want to answer?

Now break it down:

- Are you seeking knowledge, skill, or wisdom?
- What other questions will you need to answer along the way?
- Who?
- Where?
- When?
- Why?
- How?
- What?
- What else?

The second key: Identify the best sources to answer your questions. For your primary question, what are the best sources?
Now break it down:

- For each of the questions along the way, what is the best source?
- What sources have proven expertise?
- What sources are validated by independent third parties?
- What facts do you need?
- What opinions do you need?
- Do the facts make sense?
- Are they in alignment with consensus?
- Are they divergent?
- Do they make logical arguments?
- Do they acknowledge and explain other divergent facts and arguments?

Make the plan:

	Goals	Intermediate Goals	Step-by-step Checklist

Step Six: HOMEWORK OPTION. Go ahead and execute that research plan!

Proactive Learning: Lesson Plan #6 – Studying Information to Build Knowledge

Step One: Think of something you know a lot about.
Brainstorming questions:
What do you know about the subject? Make a list of what you know. How do you know it? What did you study? When did you study? Where did you study? With whom did you study? How did you study? What steps did you follow?

Step Two: Consider the following study skills:

- Memorization: Think of something you have memorized in the past. Do you still remember it? What is it? When did you memorize it? Where? With whom? How? What steps did you follow?
- Summarizing lessons from reading/listening: Think of something you have read or listened to in the past from which you have learned something valuable. Can you summarize what you learned? What did you read or to whom did you listen? When? Where? How did you go about learning what you learned? What steps did you follow?

Step Three: Make a list of your current tasks, responsibilities, and projects at work. Now take them one by one and ask yourself the following questions. What additional knowledge would really benefit you in the performance of that task, responsibility, or project? What information would be really valuable to memorize? What information would be really valuable to read or listen to and be able to summarize some concrete lessons? What is a good source from which to get that information?

Step Four: Choose one of those valuable pieces of information to memorize. Preferably it should be a piece of information that would be fun to memorize and useful to know by heart.

- Make a study sheet: Write down all the information you want to memorize.
- Take it one piece at a time.

- ◆ Read it. Close your eyes and try to recall it from memory.
- ◆ Then try to write it down from memory.
- ◆ Learn the second piece the same way.
- ◆ Then try to remember the first piece, the second piece . . . and learn the third piece.
- ◆ Then the first, second, third . . . and learn the fourth.
- ◆ And so on.
- ◆ Once you know it by heart, start using it. Keep using it.

Once you finish, choose something else that would be fun to memorize and useful to know by heart. And another. And so on.

Step Five: HOMEWORK OPTION. Choose one of those valuable pieces of information that would be good to learn from and summarize lessons. Once you finish, choose something else. And another. And so on.

Proactive Learning: Lesson Plan #7 – Practicing Technique to Build Skills

Step One: Think of something you know how to do very well – a skill. *Brainstorming questions*:

What skills do you have in this area? What do you know how to do? Make a list. How did you learn this skill? What did you practice? When did you practice? Where did you practice? With whom did you practice? How did you practice? What steps did you follow?

Step Two: Consider the following practice skills:

- ◆ Understand a technique: A technique is a precise sequence of steps with defined specifications. First you have to understand the sequence and the specifications before you can try following the sequence. Can you think of a technique you had to learn? Think about when you first learned it. Before you could practice, you had to understand, right? Understanding comes first.
- ◆ Practice the technique: Once you know what you are trying to do, you can start trying to do it. Usually practicing a precise sequence of steps with defined specifications is awkward in the initial attempts. Repetition is the key. Think of a technique you are good at. Think about when you first tried doing it. At first it was awkward, right? Repetition is the key to success.
- ◆ Getting so used to the technique, it becomes a habit. You do it without even thinking about it. That's when you have to be really careful. If you go on autopilot, almost always your skill will diminish a little bit at a time without your even noticing it. Have you ever had the experience of going on autopilot with a skill that has become a habit? Did you lose interest or have a time when you started making more mistakes? What did you learn from that experience?
- ◆ No matter how much you are in the habit, keep trying to get better; there is always room for improvement. The key to staying engaged and successful is to keep trying to get better. Have you had the experience of getting better and better and better at something? What was it? What did you learn from that?

Step Three: Make a list of your current tasks, responsibilities, and projects at work. Now take them one by one and ask yourself the following questions. What additional skill would really benefit you in the performance of that task, responsibility, or project? What techniques would be really valuable to understand and practice? What is a good source from which to get those techniques?

Step Four: Choose one of those valuable techniques to practice. Preferably it should be a technique that would be fun to practice and useful to be good at.

- Lay out the technique in a precise sequence of steps with defined specifications.
- Make sure you understand the precise sequence and the defined specifications.
- Try doing it. Let it be awkward.
- Do it again.
- And again.
- Check what you are doing against the precise sequence and the defined specifications. Break it down. Check each step. Check each specification.
- Correct your own technique.
- Do it again and again and again.
- Ask someone who is really good at it to check your technique and make corrections.
- Do it again and again and again.
- Don't stop trying to get better.

Once you finish, choose another skill to practice. And then another. And so on.

Step Five: HOMEWORK OPTION. Keep practicing!

Proactive Learning: Lesson Plan #8 – Contemplating Competing Perspectives to Build Wisdom

Step One: Think of something about which you have some real wisdom.

Brainstorming questions:

What do you understand and appreciate about the subject? Make a list of what you understand and appreciate. How many perspectives do you understand?

List all the different perspectives you can about this matter. For each one, describe the perspective, and ask yourself: How do you know it? Where did you learn it? When? From what source? With whom? What differentiates this perspective from other perspectives? What is legitimate about this perspective? What is problematic about it?

Step Two: Consider the following contemplation skills:

- First, you have to take in the perspective and understand it. That means summarizing lessons from reading/listening: Think of something you have read or listened to in the past from which you have learned something valuable. Can you summarize what you learned? What did you read or to whom did you listen? When? Where? How did you go about learning what you learned? What steps did you follow?
- Next, you want to understand the argument underlying the perspective. Learn the argument and be able to restate it. Remember a good argument follows this pattern:
  Assertion/conclusion:
  . . .is true because. . .
  Fact/source, which is important because. . .
  . . .if this fact is true, these other facts cannot be true. . .
  OR
  . . .if this fact is true, these other facts must also be true. . .
  + Fact/source, + Fact/source, etc.

- Once you understand the argument, interrogate the argument by asking it a bunch of challenging questions.
- Then seek out a very different perspective on the same subject and go through the preceding process.
- Then take another very different perspective, and another and another.

Step Three: Make a list of your current tasks, responsibilities, and projects at work. Now take them one by one and ask yourself the following questions. What additional wisdom would really benefit you in the performance of that task, responsibility, or project? What differing perspectives would be really valuable to understand? What are good sources from which to get differing perspectives?

Step Four: Choose one of those valuable pieces of wisdom. Preferably it should be a matter that would be fun to contemplate and useful to really understand better.

- Make a list of sources from which you can find differing perspectives.
- Take the sources one by one:

  Summarize the lessons
  Outline the argument
  Interrogate the argument
  Think about it

- Think about the different perspectives in relation to each other.

Once you finish this process, choose something else and do it again. And another. And so on.

Teaching Problem Solving

Problem solving: Mastering established best practices – proven, repeatable solutions for dealing with regularly recurring problems – so as to avoid reinventing the wheel. Using repeatable solutions to improvise when addressing problems that are new but similar.

BRIDGING THE GAP

In today's information environment, there are so many answers to so many questions available at the tip of our fingers. Many people today are simply not in the habit of ***really thinking*** on their feet. Without a lot of experience puzzling through problems, it should be no surprise that so many people are often puzzled when they encounter unanticipated problems.

Here's the thing. Nine out of ten times, you don't need to make important decisions on the basis of your own judgment in the moment. You are much better off if you can rely on the accumulated experience of the organization in which you are working.

Most of the problems you encounter are likely to be regularly recurring problems – even though you may have no experience with the particular problem at hand. Nonetheless, the problem has occurred before and been solved before, probably many times over. Very few of the problems you encounter should be difficult to anticipate.

Think about it. How many problems do you encounter that haven't already been solved before?

The key to teaching anybody the basics of problem solving is to anticipate the most common recurring problems and prepare with ready-made solutions. First, they will become familiar with commonly recurring problems and therefore be more likely to try to help prevent those problems, and also be less often surprised when those problems do arise. Second, they will build up a repertoire of ready-made solutions so there will be a bunch of problems they can solve without having to chase anybody down, because they will have the solution in their back pocket. Third, from learning and implementing ready-made solutions, they will learn a lot about the anatomy of a good solution. This will put them in a much better position to borrow from ready-made solutions and improvise a better solution when they do encounter the rare unanticipated problem.

Ready-made solutions are just best practices that have been cap-tured, turned into standard operating procedures, and deployed throughout the organization to employees for use as job aids. The most common job aid is a simple checklist:

If A happens, you do B
If C happens, you do D
If E happens, you do F

What kind of job aids do you have at your disposal to help your new young employees master best practices for dealing with recur-ring problems, so they don't have to "problem-solve" anew each time? If you already have such job aids at your disposal, then how can you make better use of them as learning tools? You need to get everybody using those tools. Use them to help your young employ-ees (and probably those of all ages) to anticipate and prepare for the most common problems, to build up their repertoire of ready-made solutions, and to learn the anatomy of a good solution so they are in a better position to improvise when there is truly a need for a judgment call.

Here's why you should care of about getting really good at prob-lem solving. Problems are bad. They cost time, energy, and money and they often leave people – including you – with negative feelings. Even small problems are bad because they often hide and fester and grow – and later turn into bigger problems.

The good news is that most of the problems you will encounter at work are not new problems, no matter how unfamiliar they may be to you. Most of the problems you will encounter are problems that have occurred and been solved many times before. That means we already have the ready-made solutions. All you have to do is learn them.

Ready-made solutions are very common in workplaces where problems can be very dangerous and so there is very little tolerance for error: battlefields, hospitals, airplane cockpits, nuclear weapons launch sites, and so on.

By learning and practicing ready-made step-by-step solutions, one after another, you will develop a growing list of problems for which you are well prepared with a growing repertoire of solutions. Solving problems with proven best practices is the best way to gain experience in solving problems successfully. Not only that, but by preparing in advance for regularly recurring problems, you will also be in a much better position to anticipate when those problems might occur and possibly prevent or avoid the problem altogether.

Here's the really good news: You will get better not only at solving the specific problems anticipated, but also you will get much better at solving unanticipated problems. Why is that? By learning to implement specific step-by-step solutions to recurring problems, you will learn a lot about what good problem solving looks like – like so many case studies. You will begin to understand and appreciate the common denominators and underlying principles. Over time you will learn how to draw on those common denominators and underlying principles when facing unanticipated problems. You might draw on elements of ready-made solutions, even mixing and matching to come up with solutions to unanticipated problem should the need arise to improvise.

Problem Solving: Lesson Plan #1 – Introduction

Step One: *Brainstorm*: What does "problem solving" mean to you?

Step Two: *Brainstorm*: Think of a time – inside or outside of work – when you have successfully solved a problem. What was the problem? What was the solution? How did you arrive at the solution? When did this happen? Where? Who was involved? What steps did you follow? What lesson can you draw from this experience that would help you solve similar problems in the future? What general lessons about problem solving itself can you draw from this experience that would help you solve very different kinds of problems in the future?

Step Three: *Brainstorm*: Think of someone you know – inside or outside of work – whom you consider to be very good at solving problems. Can you think of an example of a problem that you've witnessed this person solving? What was the problem? What was the solution? How did this person arrive at the solution? When did this happen? Where? Who else was involved? What steps did they follow? What lessons can you draw from this experience that would help you solve similar problems in the future? What general lessons about problem solving itself can you draw from this experience that would help you solve very different kinds of problems in the future?

Step Four: Consider the following definition of problem solving: "Problem solving: Mastering established best practices – proven repeatable solutions for dealing with regular recurring problems – so as to avoid reinventing the wheel. Using repeatable solutions to improvise when addressing problems that are new but similar." Brainstorming questions: Why is this approach to problem solving in the best interests of the organization? Why is this approach to problem solving in your best interest as an employee?

Problem Solving: Lesson Plan #2 – Preventing or Avoiding Problems Before They Happen

Step One: *Brainstorm*: Make a list of the most common recurring problems that you encounter at work.

Step Two: Now take the problems, one by one. For each one, please answer the following questions:

- ◆ When does this problem typically occur?
- ◆ Where?
- ◆ Who is typically involved?
- ◆ What happens in the typical instance of this problem?
- ◆ How does the problem usually unfold?
- ◆ Why does this problem occur?
- ◆ Can you think of steps that could be taken to prevent or avoid the problem?

Step Five: HOMEWORK OPTION. Choose one of the standard operating procedures and the corresponding tool from the previous steps. Consider trying to memorize it. If not, then at least make an effort to use it in the coming days at work. Take notes on your efforts to use it and discuss them with your manager in your next one-on-one.

Problem Solving: Lesson Plan #3 – Ready–Made Solutions to Commonly Occurring Problems

Step One: *Brainstorm*: Make a list of the most common recurring problems that you encounter at work.

Step Two: Now take the problems, one by one. For each one, please answer the following questions:

◆ Are there "official" standard operating procedures for solving this problem when it occurs?

◆ If there are standard operating procedures for solving this problem: What are the standard operating procedures? Is there a tool, such as a checklist, that contains those standard operating procedures? Do you have the tool? Do you use the tool? What can you do to make better use of it? Can you memorize it?

◆ If there is no tool, can you make a tool for yourself containing those standard operating procedures so that you can use it going forward?

◆ If there are no "official" standard operating procedures for solving this problem, then brainstorm: What are the most common "unofficial" approaches you know of? Is there a prevailing approach? Or are there multiple competing approaches? If there are multiple competing approaches, what do you think are the relative merits of the multiple competing approaches? Have you ever encountered this problem yourself? How did you solve it? What approach did you take? How did it go?

◆ If there are no "official" standard operating procedures for solving this problem, create some. Brainstorm: What do you think should be the standard operating procedures – step-by-step – for solving this problem?

Once you've developed a list of proposed standard operating procedures: Can you create a tool containing the standard operating procedures you just developed? What can you do to make sure you make good use of this tool going forward?

Step Three: What regularly occurring problems can you anticipate encountering in the coming days and weeks at work? What can you do to prepare in advance so that you will be ready to solve that problem when/if it occurs?

Step Four: HOMEWORK OPTION. Choose one of the standard operating procedures and the corresponding tool from the previous steps. Consider trying to memorize it. If not, then at least make an effort to use it in the coming days at work. Take notes on your efforts to use it and discuss them with your manager in your next one-on-one.

Problem Solving: Lesson Plan #4 – Common Denominators and Underlying Principles

Step One: Make a list of the most common recurring problems at work for which you have good standard operating procedures for preventing and/or solving the problem.

Step Two: Now, review each set of standard operating procedures, one set at a time. For each one, ask yourself:

♦ What are the general principles underlying this standard operating procedure?
♦ What do you learn from these general principles?

Keep a running list of general principles as you go through each set of standard operating procedures.

Step Three: Now carefully review the running list of general principles.

♦ What are the common denominators? The principles common to multiple sets of standard operating procedures?
♦ What do you learn from these common denominators?

Step Four: Now think of some very rarely occurring problems, problems for which there are no standard operating procedures because they are so rare. Consider how you could draw on these general principles, especially the common denominators, in order to confront these problems that are more difficult to anticipate.

Step Five: HOMEWORK OPTION. Take that list of general principles, especially the common denominators. Consider trying to memorize it. If not, then at least make an effort to use it in the coming days at work – apply those general principles to everything you do for a while. Take notes on your efforts to use it and discuss them with your manager in your next one-on-one.

Problem Solving: Lesson Plan #5 – Applying the "After-Action" Review Tool

Step One: Make a list of some real problems you've encountered at work – the more recent the better.

Step Two: Take those problems one by one. For each one, please complete what's known as an after-action review:

What actually happened, step-by-step?

When	Who	What	Where	How	Why

What actions did you take to try to avoid or prevent the problem?

Actions	Who?	Why?	Outcome

What actions did you take to try to solve the problem? Why? What was the outcome?

Actions	Who?	Why?	Outcome

What were the leading alternative actions you could have taken to avoid or prevent the problem that were not taken? What different outcomes might have occurred?

Alternative Actions	Possible Different Outcomes

What were the leading alternative actions you could have taken to solve the problem that were not taken? What different outcomes might have occurred?

Alternative Actions	Possible Different Outcomes

Step Three: Consider the after-action reviews. What do you learn from this? How can you improve?

Step Four: HOMEWORK. Consider using an after-action review tool going forward to analyze future problems when you encounter them so at least you can learn from them. If you do use the tool going forward, discuss what you learn in your one-on-one conversations with your manager.

Problem Solving: Lesson Plan #6 – Using the After-Action Review Tool to Learn from Others

Step One: Make a list of some heroic problem-solving cases you know of at work – the more recent, the better.

Step Two: Take these heroic problem-solving cases one by one. For each one, please complete what's known as an after-action review:

What actually happened, step-by-step?

When	Who	What	Where	How	Why

What actions were taken to try to avoid or prevent the problem?

Actions	Who?	Why?	Outcome

What actions were taken to try to solve the problem? Why? What was the outcome?

Actions	Who?	Why?	Outcome

Really try to break it down and spell it out so you can see exactly what actions led to the heroic problem solving.

What were the leading alternative actions that could have been taken that might have led to a less heroic outcome? What different outcomes might have occurred?

Alternative Actions	Possible Different Outcomes

Step Three: Consider the after-action reviews. What do you learn from these cases of heroic problem solving? What are the general principles? What are the common denominators?

Teaching Decision Making

Decision making: Identifying and considering multiple options, assessing the pros and cons of each, and choosing the course of action closest to the desired outcome.

BRIDGING THE GAP

Participants in our seminars sometimes ask me why I draw a distinction between "problem solving" and "decision making." Indeed, decision making could be seen as a very advanced form of problem solving. But I like to shine a bright light on this distinction: Nine out of ten problems people face in the workplace – especially the problems new young employees face – have been solved already. Usually the best way to solve a problem is to take a good repeatable solution from the past and apply it in the moment. That's why our approach to problem solving is nine-tenths about capturing and learning repeatable solutions so as to prepare in advance for the recurring problem. Decision making, on the other hand, is for that rare breed of problem – or that sliver (more or less) present in every problem – where the decision has not been made already by someone with more experience and authority.

Think about that sliver of any problem where you have to decide what the problem really is in the first place.

What is the essence of decision making anyway? It's not the same thing as sheer brain power, mental capacity, or natural intelligence. It's not a matter of accumulated knowledge or memorized information. It is more than the mastery of techniques and tools.

If you think of decision making, maybe you think of the most basic decision-making tool, the weighing of pros and cons. But pros and cons are really just predictions of likely outcomes. So your pros and cons list is useless if you can't accurately predict the likely outcomes of one choice versus another.

Good decision making is really about being able to predict likely outcomes – the ability to see the connections between cause and effect – to project out the consequences of one set of events and actions as opposed to another. The irony is that the only way to develop that "go forward" ability to predict the future is to learn from the past.

But experience alone does not teach good decision making. The key to learning from experience is paying close attention and aggressively drawing lessons from your experiences. If you can begin to see the patterns in causes and their effects, then you can start to think ahead with insight. Ultimately, that's the key to decision making.

Here's why you should care of about getting really good at decision making. Decision making is a very high-level skill that is very hard to develop without years of experience. But you can accelerate the learning curve.

The key is learning to understand the connection between cause and effect so that you can learn to predict the future.

How does it work?

In retrospect, the key is working backward from effects to assess likely causes, to figure out what decisions and actions led to the current situation. That means being really aggressive about learning from your own experiences.

This is the essence of the lessons-learned process that is ubiquitous in the military and intelligence agencies. Every mission is subjected to intense scrutiny immediately after the fact. Leaders at all levels involved in a mission are expected to go over every decision and action, step-by-step, to determine exactly what happened and why. Then they meet to discuss and debate these decisions and actions. They call it an after-action review.

You want to learn to apply this process to every "mission" you undertake at work, to every move you make at work. Do you stop and reflect after making decisions and taking actions? Do you stop and reflect on outcomes and consequences? Do you look at outcomes and consequences and trace them back to see the chains of cause and effect? What actually happened, step-by-step? What decisions were made? What actions were taken? What different outcomes might have occurred?

Going forward, the key to getting good at decision making is learning to think ahead and accurately project the likely outcomes and consequences of specific decisions and actions.

Have you ever played chess or any other game of strategy? The key to success in any game of strategy is thinking ahead. Before making a move, you play out in your head the likely outcomes, often over a long sequence of moves and countermoves. If I do A, the other player would probably respond with B. Then I would do C, and he would probably respond with D. Then I would do E, and he would probably respond with F. And so on. This is what strategic planners call a decision/action-tree because each decision or action is the beginning of a branch of responses and counterresponses. In fact, each decision or action creates a series of possible responses, and each possible response creates a series of possible counterresponse.

You want to learn to think ahead and play out the likely sequence of moves and countermoves in everything you do. Do you think about cause and effect? Do you stop and reflect before making decisions and taking actions? Do you project likely outcomes in advance? Do you look at each decision and action as a set of choices, each with identifiable consequences?

Decision Making: Lesson Plan #1 – Introduction

Step One: *Brainstorm*: What does "decision making" mean to you?

Step Two: *Brainstorm*: Think of a time – inside or outside of work – when you have made a good decision. What was the decision? What were your options? How did you weigh the competing options? Ultimately how did you make your decision? What were the outcomes/ consequences? When did this happen? Where? Who was involved? What steps did you follow? What lesson can you draw from this experience that would help you make good decisions in the future?

Step Three: *Brainstorm*: Think of a time – inside or outside of work – when you have made a decision that turned out to be a bad one. What was the decision? What were your options? How did you weigh the competing options? Ultimately how did you make your decision? What were the outcomes/consequences? When did this happen? Where? Who was involved? What steps did you follow? What lesson can you draw from this experience that would help you avoid making bad decisions like this one in the future?

Step Four: *Brainstorm*: Think of someone you know – inside or outside of work – whom you consider to be very good at making decisions. Can you think of an example of a decision you've witnessed this person making? What was the decision? What were the competing options? Ultimately how did this person make the decision? What were the outcomes/consequences? When did this happen? Where? Who else was involved? What steps did this person follow? What lessons can you draw from this experience that would help you make good decisions in the future?

Step Five: *Brainstorm*: Think of someone you know – inside or outside of work – whom you consider to make bad decisions. Can you think of an example of a decision you've witnessed this person making? What was the decision? What were the competing options? Ultimately how did this person make the decision? What were the outcomes/consequences? When did this happen? Where? Who else was involved? What steps did the this person follow? What lessons can you draw from this experience that would help you avoid making bad decisions in the future?

Step Six: Consider the following definition of decision making: "Decision making: Identifying and considering multiple options, assessing the pros and cons of each, and choosing the course of action closest to the desired outcome."

   Brainstorming questions:

   Why is this approach to decision making in the best interests of the organization? Why is this approach to decision making in your best interest as an employee?

Decision Making: Lesson Plan #2 – Information Analysis: Simple Pros and Cons

Step One: *Brainstorm*: Think of an important decision that you need to make – inside or outside of work.

Or else take one of the choice sets below and use that "decision" to be made as your case study. In each of the following choice sets, imagine you must make a mutually exclusive decision: If you could only choose one or the other, "Would you rather. . ."

> . . .get paid more money or have more time off?
> . . .disappoint an important customer or disappoint an important vendor?
> . . .impress your boss or impress your direct reports?
> . . .improve the quality of your work or improve your productivity?
> . . .improve the quality of our products or lower the price?
> . . .love your work or win prestigious accolades for your work?

Or think of another set of choices to use as your example for the following steps.

Step Two: Now consider the decision to be made and the options before you:

- ◆ What do you know? What don't you know?
- ◆ What else should you know in order to make a good decision?
- ◆ Do you need to do some research before considering your options?
  - If so, what are your research questions? And. . .
  - What are your best sources for answering those questions?

Step Three: Before considering your options, you need to consider what's at stake in making this decision. Answer these questions:

- ◆ Why is a decision required?
- ◆ When does the decision need to be made?

- What are your goals in making the decision?
- Who else will or might be affected by the decision?
- What stands to gain? Who stands to lose?
- What rules/principles should you follow in making the decision?

Step Four: Now consider your options. List all of your options. What are all the logical possibilities in this situation?

Step Five: Take all of your options, one by one. For each option, start by making an exhaustive pros and cons list for each option. Of course, not all pros and cons are of the same weight. Take note.

Step Six: Now for each option, make the strongest argument in favor and the strongest argument against.

Remember a good argument follows this pattern:

Assertion/conclusion:

. . .is true *because*. . .

Fact/source, which is important *because*. . .

. . .if this fact is true, these other facts cannot be true. . .

OR

. . .if this fact is true, these other facts must also be true. . .

+ Fact/source, + Fact/source, etc.

Step Seven: What are your strongest options? Make a decision.

Decision Making: Lesson Plan #3 – Cause and Effect: Positive Outcomes

Step One: *Brainstorm*: Make a list of positive outcomes and consequences that you encounter at work. Consider examples of

- Happy customers
- Happy employees
- Happy vendors
- Delivering services or products
- Adding value by making things smarter, faster, or better
- Solving problems
- Identifying opportunities
- Making money
- Feeling useful

Step Two: Now take your list of positive outcomes/consequences at work, one by one. For each one, please answer the following questions:

- What causes this positive outcome/consequence?
  - Who is involved?
  - When does it happen?
  - How?
  - Where?
  - What happens?
  - Why does it happen?

Step Three: Again, take the positive outcomes/consequences one by one. For each one, tell the story based on the answers to the questions above. What is the story of how that positive outcome/consequence came to be?

Step Four: Again, for each of the positive outcomes/consequences: What decisions were made along the way? Who made those decisions? What options did this person have? How could a different decision have resulted in a less positive outcome/consequence?

Step Five: What lessons do you learn from this?

Decision Making: Lesson Plan #4 – Cause and Effect: Negative Outcomes

Step One: *Brainstorm*: Make a list of negative outcomes and consequences that you might encounter at work. Consider examples of

- Unhappy customers
- Unhappy employees
- Unhappy vendors
- Failing to deliver on services or products
- Making errors in work or failing to get enough done
- Causing problems
- Missing opportunities
- Losing money
- Feeling bad about the role you play at work

Step Two: Now take your list of negative outcomes/consequences at work, one by one. For each one, please answer the following questions:

- What causes this negative outcome/consequence?
  - Who is involved?
  - When does it happen?
  - How?
  - Where?
  - What happens?
  - Why does it happen?

Step Three: Again, take the negative outcomes/consequences one by one. For each one, tell the story based on the answers to the questions above. What is the story of how that negative outcome/consequence came to be?

Step Four: Again, for each of the negative outcomes/consequences: What decisions were made along the way? Who made those decisions? What options did this person have? How could a different decision have resulted in a more positive outcome/consequence?

Step Five: What lessons do you learn from this? What causes should be avoided? What decisions should not be made?

Decision Making: Lesson Plan #5 – Applying the After-Action Review Tool

Step One: Make a list of some real decisions you have encountered at work – the more recent, the better.

Step Two: Take those decisions, one by one. For each one, please complete an after-action review:

What decision was made? Who made it? Why? What was the outcome?

Decisions	Who?	Why?	Outcome

What actions were taken? Who made them? Why? What was the outcome?

Actions	Who?	Why?	Outcome

What were the leading alternative decisions that were not made? What different outcomes might have occurred?

Alternative Decisions	Possible Different Outcomes

What were the leading alternative actions that were not taken? What different outcomes might have occurred?

Alternative Actions	Possible Different Outcomes

Step Three: Consider the after-action reviews. What do you learn from this?

Step Four: HOMEWORK. Consider using an after-action review tool going forward to analyze future decisions when you encounter them so at least you can learn from them. If you do use the tool going forward, discuss what you learn in your one-on-one conversations with your manager.

Decision Making: Lesson Plan #6 – Using the "Decision/Action Tree"

Step One: Make a list of some real decisions you anticipate encountering at work in the coming days or weeks.

Step Two: Take those decisions, one by one. For each one, think ahead. . .

- ◆ What are all of your options?
- ◆ For each option, complete the following decision/action tree:
  - • If you take this decision/action, who is likely to respond, how, when, where, and why?
  - • What set of options will this cut off?
  - • What set of options will this create?
- ◆ For each option, keep going:
  - • If you take this decision/action, who is likely to respond, how, when, where, and why?
  - • What set of options will this cut off?
  - • What set of options will this create?
- ◆ For each option, keep going:
  - • If you take this decision/action, who is likely to respond, how, when, where, and why?
  - • What set of options will this cut off?
  - • What set of options will this create?

Step Three: Consider your decision/action trees. What do you learn from this?

Step Four: HOMEWORK. Consider using a decision/action tree going forward to analyze future decisions when you encounter them. If you do use the tool going forward, discuss what you learn in your one-on-one conversations with your manager.

Step Five: HOMEWORK. Get your hands on one or more of the following famous books about strategy:

Sun Tzu, *The Art of War*

Miyamito Mushashi, *The Book of Five Rings*

Nicolo Machiavelli, *The Prince*

HBR, *Must Reads on Strategy*

As you read each one, keep a written journal of lessons.

Chapter 6

Teaching the Missing Basics of Teamwork

Teamwork: The Missing Basics

- ◆ Respect for context: Reading and adapting to the existing structure, rules, customs, and leadership in an unfamiliar situation.
- ◆ Citizenship: Accepting, embracing, and observing, not just the rights and rewards, but the duties of membership, belonging, and participation in a defined group with its own structure, rules, customs, and leadership.
- ◆ Service: Approaching relationships in terms of what you have to offer – respect, commitment, hard work, creativity, sacrifice – rather than what you need or want.
- ◆ Playing your position: Doing the part assigned (or relegated) to you to support the larger mission; coordinating, cooperating, and collaborating with others in pursuit of a shared goal; supporting and celebrating the success of others.

Teaching Respect for Context

Respect for context: Reading and adapting to the existing structure, rules, customs, and leadership in an unfamiliar situation.

BRIDGING THE GAP

Before individuals can possibly succeed at practicing good "teamwork," they must develop a fundamental respect for context. They must learn to read and appreciate and accept and embrace adapting to the existing structure, rules, customs, and leaders in an unfamiliar situation.

Indeed, employees today are more and more likely to disagree openly with employers' missions, policies, and decisions and to challenge employment conditions and established reward systems. They are less obedient to employers' rules and supervisors' instructions. They are less likely to heed organizational chart authority.

Increasingly, workers respect transactional authority: control of resources, control of rewards, and control of work conditions. There are really only two ways you can choose to go in a new job: fit in or stand out. Too often, people have the inclination to stand out.

Managers often tell us that today's new young employees seem to suffer from a fundamental lack of context. Yes, this is partly a function of youth; younger people have less life experience than older people and thus fewer points of reference to compare circumstances, people, and relationships. Context is all about these points of reference. So, lack of context goes with being in the first adult life stages. But there is much more going on here.

Our research indicates that people of all ages today are less likely to appreciate and accept and defer to the existing context of systems and practices of an organization/team, even if they are relatively new to an established organization/team.

The good news is that employment is, ultimately, a transactional relationship. The employer is the customer. Just in this context:

> In this role in this job in this chain of command in this organization, if you want to belong here, this is how you understand, accept, embrace, and adapt to your place in the structure, rules, customers, and leadership here.

Developing appreciation and respect for context means realizing that work is situational and employees' roles in any situation is determined in large part by factors that have nothing to do with them. There are preexisting, independent factors that would be present even if they were not, and those factors determine the context of any situation.

The easiest way to understand context is to consider extreme examples of it: dire illness, hurricanes, war, etc. In any of these contexts, the possibilities are limited, and so is the scope of an individual's potential role. In these contexts, certain expectations, hopes, expressions, and actions are inappropriate. While it is relatively easy to be sensitive to extreme contexts, it is often difficult to be sensitive to more subtle contexts, particularly when we walk into new situations. Every situation has a context that limits possibilities and limits the scope of an individual's potential role.

If you want to be set up for success in any situation, step one is learning to read and adapt to the existing structure, rules, customs, and leaders in that situation.

Here's why you as an employee should care about learning to read and adapt to a new context – and this context in particular.

No matter who you are, what you want to achieve, or how you want to behave, your role in any work situation is determined in large part by factors that have nothing to do with you. Every situation has a context that limits possibilities and limits the scope of your potential role.

Once you get a handle on the context of your work situation, next you have to ask yourself where you fit in this context. Why are you here? What is at stake for you? When did you get here? What is your appropriate role in relation to the other people in the group? What is your appropriate role in relation to the mission? What expectations and hopes are reasonable for you to have?

Once you really understand your role in any work context, then your number one responsibility is to play that role to the absolute best of your ability. That means, contribute your very best, and put in more time and effort no matter how lowly, mundane, or repetitive your tasks and responsibilities might seem in relation to the overall mission of your organization.

Respect for Context: Lesson Plan #1 – Introduction

Step One: Consider: What does it mean to you to show "respect for context" in an unfamiliar situation?

Step Two: Consider the following definition of "respect for context": "Reading and adapting to the existing structure, rules, customs, and leaders in an unfamiliar situation."

Brainstorm: Why is this approach to context in the best interests of the organization – your current employer? Why is this approach to context in your best interests as an employee? Are there good reasons to reject this approach to context?

Step Three: Now consider the context of this particular workplace. How can you "read and adapt" to this context? Describe in as much detail as you can:

	Read	Adapt
. . .the structure. . .		
. . .the rules. . .		
. . .the customs. . .		
. . .the leadership. . .		

Respect for Context: Lesson Plan #2 – Reading the Structure, Rules, Customs, Leadership

This exercise can be done as a solitary exercise using just this written questionnaire. Alternatively you can facilitate the completion by individuals – solo or in a group – by reading them through the questionnaire as they respond in writing individually. As a third option, this exercise can also be used for a group discussion.

Step One: Consider the context of this particular workplace. How do you "read" this context? Describe in as much detail as you can:

> . . .the structure. . .
> . . .the rules. . .
> . . .the customs. . .
> . . .the leadership. . .

Step Two: Consider the structure of this workplace. "Read" it.
Brainstorm:

- What do you know?
- What don't you know or understand?
- What do you need to know or understand better?
- How can you learn? What resources and support do you need?

Step Three: Consider the rules of this workplace. "Read" them.
Brainstorm:

- What do you know?
- What don't you know or understand?
- What do you need to know or understand better?
- How can you learn? What resources and support do you need?

Step Four: Consider the customs of this workplace. "Read" them.
Brainstorm:

- What do you know?
- What don't you know or understand?

- ◆ What do you need to know or understand better?
- ◆ How can you learn? What resources and support do you need?

Step Five: Consider the leadership of this workplace. "Read" it. *Brainstorm:*

- ◆ What do you know?
- ◆ What don't you know or understand?
- ◆ What do you need to know or understand better?
- ◆ How can you learn? What resources and support do you need?

Respect for Context: Lesson Plan #3 – Where Do You Fit?

Step One: *Brainstorm*: Consider the context of this workplace. Where do you "fit" in this context? Ask yourself:

◆ Where am I? What is this place?
◆ What is going on here? What is the mission of the group?
◆ Why is everybody here? What is at stake for the group and for each person in the group?
◆ When did they all get here?
◆ Who are all these people? What role does each person play?
◆ How are they accustomed to doing things around here? What is standard operating procedure?
◆ Why am I here?
◆ What is at stake for me?
◆ When did I get here?
◆ What is my appropriate role in relation to the other people in the group?
◆ What is my appropriate role in relation to the mission? Who am I in this context?

Step Two: *Brainstorm*: Consider the structure of this workplace. Where do you "fit" in this structure?

Step Three: *Brainstorm*: Consider the rules of this workplace. Where do you "fit" in relation to the rules?

Step Four: *Brainstorm*: Consider the customs of this workplace. Where do you "fit" in relation to the customs?

Step Five: *Brainstorm*: Consider the leadership of this workplace. Where do you "fit" in relation to the leadership this context?

Respect for Context: Lesson Plan #4 – What Do You Need to Do to Adapt?

Step One: *Brainstorm*: Consider the context of this workplace. What do you need to do to "adapt" to this context?

Step Two: *Brainstorm*: Consider the structure of this workplace. What do you need to do to adapt to the structure of this workplace?

Step Three: *Brainstorm*: Consider the rules of this workplace. What do you need to do to adapt to the rules of this workplace?

Step Four: *Brainstorm*: Consider the customs of this workplace. What do you need to do to adapt to the customs of this workplace?

Step Five: *Brainstorm*: Consider the leadership of this workplace. What do you need to do to adapt to the leadership of this workplace?

Respect for Context: Lesson Plan #5 – Context-Limiting Factors

Step One: Consider each of the following context-limiting factors one by one. For each factor, describe how the factor can shape the context.

- Resource constraints – insufficient information, people, material, or tools
- Limited time
- Too much work
- Other people not doing their part
- Things are constantly changing
- Competing priorities
- Distance
- Weather
- Company policies, rules, regulations, and procedures
- The way things have always been done around here
- Too many low-priority distractions
- Interruptions
- Conflict between and among employees
- My manager is often unavailable
- Unclear lines of authority
- I answer to too many different people
- Inconsistency from one manager to another

Step Two: Consider each of the factors again, one by one. For each one: Can you think of examples of when you have been in this context? Did you read and adapt to the context well? How could you have read and adapted to the context better?

Step Three: Consider each of the factors again. For each one: Can you anticipate being in this situation again in the future? When is that likely to happen? Where? Who might be involved? What do you think is likely to happen? What options will you have? How will you adapt?

Respect for Context: Lesson Plan #6 – Complicated Relationships

Step One: Certain relationship dynamics in the workplace are more complicated than others. Consider the following complicated relationship dynamics:

♦ The multiple boss problem: Do you answer to more than one boss?

♦ The chain-of-command problem: Is it clear to you exactly who is your immediate boss?

♦ Older, more experienced colleagues

♦ Conflicts, dislikes, and gripes between and among employees

♦ Friendships, cliques, and other relationships at work

♦ Interdependency with employees in other teams, departments, or divisions, or even outside vendors

List any other complicated relationship dynamics you might have dealt with in the workplace.

Step Two: Consider each of the complicated relationship dynamics one by one. For each one: Can you think of examples of when you have dealt with this dynamic? Did you read and adapt to the context well? How could you have read and adapted to the context better?

Step Three: Consider each of the dynamics again. For each one: Can you anticipate being in this situation again in the future? When is that likely to happen? Where? Who might be involved? What do you think is likely to happen? What options will you have? How will you read and adapt to the context?

Respect for Context: Lesson Plan #7 – Positive Contexts

Step One: Consider the following positive workplace contexts:

- Positive context #1.
  Working primarily on tasks and responsibilities that you enjoy and are particularly good at.

- Positive context #2.
  Being able to balance your time at work with free time. Rest, recover, relax, and rejuvenate in between times you must work.

- Positive context # 3.
  When you work with people you like and respect. Avoid people you find "toxic" and stick to those you appreciate.

- Positive context #4.
  Working in a workspace that is comfortable and in a location that you enjoy. If only!

- Positive context #5.
  Leaving your non-work issues at the door when you arrive at work.

Step Two: Consider each of the positive workplace contexts one by one. For each one: Can you think of examples of when you have been in this situation? Did you read and adapt to the context well? How could you have read and adapted to the context better?

Step Three: Consider the positive contexts again. For each one: Can you anticipate being in this situation again in the future? When is that likely to happen? Where? Who might be involved? What do you think is likely to happen? What options will you have? How will you read and adapt to the context optimally?

Respect for Context: Lesson Plan #8 – Negative Contexts

Step One: Consider the following negative workplace contexts:

- ◆ Negative context #1.
  When the work is not necessarily work that you enjoy or excel at.

- ◆ Negative context #2.
  When you barely have time to think, much less rest.

- ◆ Negative context #3.
  When you have to deal with so many people whom you probably would not choose as your colleagues – including the toxic.

- ◆ Negative context #4.
  Being physically uncomfortable at work and stuck in a location that is not your preference.

- ◆ Negative context #5.
  When things might be problematic in your personal life and it is very hard to leave those issues at the door when you arrive at work.

Step Two: Consider each of the negative workplace contexts one by one. For each one: Can you think of examples of when you have been in this situation? Did you read and adapt to the context well? How could you have read and adapted to the context better?

Step Three: Consider the negative contexts again. For each one: Can you anticipate being in this situation again in the future? When is that likely to happen? Where? Who might be involved? What do you think is likely to happen? What options will you have? How will you read and adapt to the context optimally?

Respect for Context: Lesson Plan #9 – Dealing with People with Bad Attitudes

Step One: Some people are harder to deal with in the workplace than others. Consider the following "bad attitude" types:

- "Porcupines"
  Porcupines send the message: "Get away from me!"

- "Entanglers"
  Entanglers want everybody else to be involved in their issues – they want to be noticed, observed, listened to, and engaged – even if those issues are not the concern of the person in question.

- "Debaters"
  Debaters always have an argument to make, regardless of whether it is a good argument or not.

- "Complainers"
  Complainers point out the negative symptoms of a situation without offering a solution based on the root cause.

- "Blamers"
  Blamers are like complainers in that they point out negative symptoms, but blamers also point the finger at a specific individual.

- "Stink bomb throwers"
  Stink bomb throwers make sarcastic (or worse) remarks, curse under their breath (or aloud), or even make loud gestures such as slamming or yelling.

Step Two: Consider each of these types. For each one: Can you think of examples of when you have dealt with someone behaving this way? Did you read and adapt to the context well? How could you have read and adapted to the context better?

Step Three: Consider each of the types again. For each one: Can you anticipate being in this situation again in the future? When is that likely to happen? Where? Who might be involved? What do you think is likely to happen? What options will you have? How will you read and adapt to the context?

Respect for Context: Lesson Plan #10 – Dealing with People with "Great" Attitudes

Step One: Some people are much easier to deal with in the workplace than others. Consider the following "great attitude" types:

- When you are dealing with someone who is approachable, welcoming, and professional?
- When you are dealing with someone who communicates in a highly purposeful manner – brief, straightforward, and efficient?
- When you are dealing with someone who chooses their arguments carefully, and makes arguments based on clear evidence, rather than assertions of opinion?
- When you are dealing with someone who is a good troubleshooter, placing the focus on what steps they can take personally to make things better?
- When you are dealing with someone who goes out of their way to make positive, optimistic, generous comments? Speak in positive tones? Make positive gestures and expressions?

Step Two: Consider each of these types. For each one: Can you think of examples of when you have dealt with someone behaving this way? Did you read and adapt to the context well? How could you have read and adapted to the context better?

Step Three: Consider each of the types again. For each one: Can you anticipate being in this situation again in the future? When is that likely to happen? Where? Who might be involved? What do you think is likely to happen? What options will you have? How will you read and adapt to the context?

Teaching Citizenship

Citizenship: Accepting, embracing, and observing, not just the rights, but the duties of membership, belonging, and participation in a defined group with its own structure, rules, customs, and leaders.

BRIDGING THE GAP

Is loyalty dead?

For many years in our research, we've been asking people of all ages, "Are you loyal to your employer?"

Most would assume that the oldest, most experienced people would probably evince the most employee loyalty, while the youngest, least experienced, would be the most disloyal employees. The conventional wisdom says that employee loyalty has been diminishing steadily from one generation to the next; from the Boomers to Generation X to the Millennials and now to Generation Z and beyond. Funny enough, our research shows just the opposite. The older the person, the more likely they are to say, "No." The younger the person, the more likely they are to say "Yes." That no longer surprises me. The reason is that the very meaning of employee loyalty is changing.

What today's young people mean when they say they are "loyal" to their employer is the kind of loyalty you get in a marketplace. It's the kind of loyalty you give to a customer; you get exactly as much loyalty as you pay for and it lasts as long as you keep paying.

No hard feelings to you, the employer. It's just not about you. It's about them. Every step of the way, today's employees are going to try to fit their work situation into the life experience they are trying to create for themselves. The thing is that, in the earlier life and career stages, especially in these times, what's going on in their lives at any given moment is not so easy to assess. And it is often a moving target:

- ◆ Sometimes workers just want a place to hide out and collect a paycheck. I call that *just a job*.
- ◆ Sometimes workers are taking stock and trying to figure out what they really want to do next. I call this a *weigh station job*.
- ◆ Sometimes workers look at work as a place to hang out with friends. I call this a *peer group job*.

- ◆ Sometimes workers find a job opportunity that aligns with their deep interests and priorities.
- ◆ Sometimes workers see a job as an opportunity to work like crazy for a period of time with the chance of a giant payoff.
- ◆ Sometimes what a person might value in a job is an unusual opportunity to meet an idiosyncratic need or want. It might be to work a very particular schedule, or work with particular individuals, or work in a particular location, or learn a particular skill, or do a particular task, or engage in some non-work activity (sleeping or reading or watching television) on the job. I call this a *needle-in-a-haystack job*.
- ◆ The very best case is what I refer to as a *self-building job*. This is when workers look at the job as a chance to make an impact while building themselves up with your resources. They hope to learn, grow, and collect proof of their ability to add value. As long as you keep supporting their self-building, this will bring out their best for the most sustained period.

This is very frustrating to a lot of employers. Managers often point to this unwillingness among employees to make personal sacrifices without a clear quid pro quo, without asking, "What's in it for me?" To the ears of many older, more experienced people, this sounds a lot like disloyalty, which is sort of like the opposite of good citizenship. The whole idea of "citizenship" is that it is something more – there is an intangible element – a selflessness that goes beyond the transactional relationship.

Here's what I always tell managers: "Let go of the idea that good citizenship has to be completely selfless." Good citizenship does not require selflessness. It's ok if there is a quid pro quo. Employment relationships are transactional by nature. There are very few people going to work every day who do not need to make a living. Most people would stop coming to work if you stopped paying them. That does not make them disloyal. You can get a very deep level of true commitment – something more – and still have the essence of the relationship be transactional.

Membership, belonging, and participation comes with rights and rewards – that is the quid pro quo. What good citizenship requires is this: When you "join," you are also fully accepting, embracing, and promising to observe the duties – even at considerable personal sacrifice – that are on the other side of that quid pro quo. That means you have to define those duties in no uncertain terms and make it really clear why they are important.

Over time, the power of belonging comes more and more from accepting, embracing, and observing your duties than it does from enjoying the rights and rewards of membership. But that's one of those secrets of wisdom that only comes with experience and age.

Here's why you should care about learning to be a great citizen of this organization. Working here is very valuable. Joining this organization comes with a lot of rewards. But the rewards of membership – the rewards of belonging – also go along with considerable duties.

What good citizenship requires is this: When you "join" an organization like this one, you need to be prepared to accept and embrace and observe the duties – even sometimes at considerable personal sacrifice – that go along with all the rewards.

Like every workplace, this organization has its own structure, rules, customs, and leadership. What good citizenship means in one organization may be very different from what it means in another.

What does this mean for you? First, it means you need to know what really matters to you. What is "in it for you" here in this job? And what is that worth to you? Second, it means you need to understand our structure, rules, customs, and leadership and what that requires of you. You need to really understand what it means to be a good workplace citizen in this organization. Third, you need to make sure you feel really great about accepting, embracing, and observing the duties of belonging here – the duties of what it means to be a good workplace citizen here – along with the rewards.

Good citizenship means different things to different people. But it really matters. Being a bad citizen is one of the worst things you can be. Even if you are good at your job, if the powers that be consider you "disloyal" or somehow dishonorable in terms of fulfilling your duties as an employee – that is, not just "doing your job" but doing it like a good citizen should. It is not always tangible. That's why it can be so hard to teach. Yet those intangible elements of performance really matter. So do your best to make them as tangible as you possibly can.

Good Citizenship: Lesson Plan #1 – Introduction

Step One: Brainstorm: What does "good citizenship" mean to you?

Step Two: Consider the following definition of "good citizenship": "Accepting, embracing, and observing, not just the rights and rewards, but the duties of membership, belonging, and participation in a defined group with its own structure, rules, customs, and leadership."

Brainstorm: Why is this approach to citizenship in the best interests of the organization? Why is this approach to citizenship in your best interests as an employee? Are there good reasons to reject this approach to citizenship?

Step Three: Now consider the rights and rewards of being an employee in this organization.

Brainstorm: What are the rights and rewards which benefit you as an employee here? What does it mean to accept, embrace, and observe those rights and rewards?

Step Four: Consider the other side of the equation.

Brainstorm: What does it mean to be a "good citizen" – as an employee – in this organization? What are your duties as a good citizen? Go beyond just "doing your job." Exactly HOW does a good citizen in this organization go about "doing your job"?

- ◆ Are there formal requirements?
- ◆ Are there informal requirements?
- ◆ What are the parameters among those who are considered "good citizens"?
- ◆ What should be the parameters of "good citizenship" in this organization?

Step Five: Now make a list of the duties of good citizenship as an employee in this organization.

Step Six: Now consider the list of duties, one by one. For each one: Can you think of examples of individuals exemplifying good citizenship by accepting, embracing, and observing these duties? What does it mean for you to accept, embrace, and observe those duties?

Step Seven: Now go through the list of duties and define each of the duties of citizenship with bullet points or short sentences.

Step Eight: Consider each of the duties of citizenship as defined, one by one. For each one: How are you doing personally when it comes to fulfilling this duty of good citizenship? Are you performing at 100%? If not, then what percentage would you give your performance? Where is the gap? What do you need to do to improve?

Good Citizenship: Lesson Plan #2 – The "Respect" for Others Model

Step One: Consider the following model of "good workplace citizenship."

- Respect for other people's time.
- Respect for other people's workspace.
- Respect for other people's knowledge and experience.
- Respect for other people's labor.
- Respect for other people's resources.
- Respect for other people's ideas and creativity.
- Respect for other people's relationships at work.
- Respect for other people's well-being.

Step Two: What do you think of this model?

Brainstorm: Why might this approach to citizenship be in the best interests of the organization? Why might this approach to citizenship be in your best interests as an employee? What happens when "respecting" one of these things is inconsistent with "respecting" another?

Step Three: Consider each of the "best practices" or duties in this model, one by one. For each, answer the following questions: Can you think of examples of individuals exemplifying good citizenship in this way? What would it mean for you? Define each of these "best practices" or duties with bullet points or short sentences.

Step Four: Now once again consider each of the duties in this model, as you've defined them. For each, answer the following questions:

- How are people in our organization (or team) overall doing when it comes to this approach to good citizenship? What can we do to get better?
- How are you doing as an individual when it comes to this approach? What can you do to get better?

Step Five: HOMEWORK. Consider bringing this model forward with you into your day-to-day work. Try to be a better citizen, according to this model. Keep track of how you are doing in writing. Talk about it with your manager in your one-on-ones.

Good Citizenship: Lesson Plan #3 – The "Best Interests" Model

Step One: Consider the following model of "good workplace citizenship."

- Do what's best for the mission.
- Do what's best for the company.
- Do what's best for the customers.
- Do what's best for the employees.
- Do what's best for our partners and vendors.
- Do what's best for our community.

Step Two: What do you think of this model?

Brainstorm: Why might this approach to citizenship be in the best interests of the organization? Why might this approach to citizenship be in your best interests as an employee? What happens when "what's best" for one is inconsistent with "what's best" for another?

Step Three: Consider each of the "best practices" or duties in this model, one by one. For each, answer the following questions: Can you think of examples of individuals exemplifying good citizenship in this way? What would it mean for you? Define each of these "best practices" or duties with bullet points or short sentences.

Step Four: Now once again consider each of the duties in this model, as you've defined them. For each, answer the following questions:

- How are people in our organization (or team) overall doing when it comes to this approach to good citizenship? What can we do to get better?
- How are you doing as an individual when it comes to this approach? What can you do to get better?

Step Five: HOMEWORK. Consider bringing this model forward with you into your day-to-day work. Try to be a better citizen, according to this model. Keep track of how you are doing in writing. Talk about it with your manager in your one-on-ones.

Good Citizenship: Lesson Plan #4 – The "Civic" Model

Step One: Consider the following model of "good citizenship."

- Deliberating civilly
- Monitoring and reporting on activities of decision makers
- Building coalitions
- Managing conflicts fairly and without violence
- Petitioning, documenting, speaking, and providing evidence and arguments in favor and against different positions

Step Two: What do you think of this model?

Brainstorm: Why might this approach to citizenship be in the best interests of the organization? Why might this approach to citizenship be in your best interests as an employee? What are the downsides of this more "civic" way of thinking about citizenship?

Step Three: Consider each of the "best practices" or duties in this model, one by one. For each, answer the following questions: Can you think of examples of individuals exemplifying good citizenship in this way? What would it mean for you? Define each of the "best practices" or duties above with bullet points or short sentences.

Step Four: Now once again consider each of the duties in this model, as you've defined them. For each, answer the following questions:

- How are people in our organization (or team) overall doing when it comes to this approach to good citizenship? What can we do to get better?
- How are you doing as an individual when it comes to this approach? What can you do to get better?

Step Five: HOMEWORK. Consider bringing this model forward with you into your day-to-day work. Try to be a better citizen, according to this model. Keep track of how you are doing in writing. Talk about it with your manager in your one-on-ones.

Good Citizenship: Lesson Plan #5 – The "Communitarian" Model

Step One: Consider the following model of values-oriented "good citizenship."

- ◆ Honesty
- ◆ Compassion
- ◆ Respect
- ◆ Responsibility
- ◆ Courage

Step Two: What do you think of this model?

Brainstorm: Why might this approach to citizenship be in the best interests of the organization? Why might this approach to citizenship be in your best interests as an employee? What are the downsides?

Step Three: Consider each of the "best practices" or duties in this model, one by one. For each, answer the following questions: Can you think of examples of individuals exemplifying good citizenship in this way? What would it mean for you? Define each of the "best practices" or duties above with bullet points or short sentences.

Step Four: Now once again consider each of the duties in this model, as you've defined them. For each, answer the following questions:

- ◆ How are people in our organization (or team) overall doing when it comes to this approach to good citizenship? What can we do to get better?
- ◆ How are you doing as an individual when it comes to this approach? What can you do to get better?

Step Five: HOMEWORK. Consider bringing this model forward with you into your day-to-day work. Try to be a better citizen, according to this model. Keep track of how you are doing in writing. Talk about it with your manager in your one-on-ones.

Good Citizenship: Lesson Plan #6 – The "Common Sense" Model

Step One: Consider the following model of "good citizenship."

♦ Exhibit respect, kindness, courtesy, and good manners.
♦ Prepare in advance before meetings or one-on-one conversations so that you are brief, direct, and clear.
♦ Never speak of a problem unless you have thought of at least one potential solution.
♦ Take personal responsibility for everything you say and do.
♦ Don't make excuses when you make a mistake.
♦ Don't blame or complain.
♦ Don't take yourself too seriously.
♦ Always take your commitments and responsibilities seriously.
♦ Always give people credit for their achievements, no matter how small.

Step Two: What do you think of this model?
Brainstorm: Why might this approach to citizenship be in the best interests of the organization? Why might this approach to citizenship be in your best interests as an employee? What are the downsides?

Step Three: Consider each of the "best practices" or duties in this model, one by one. For each, answer the following questions: Can you think of examples of individuals exemplifying good citizenship in this way? What would it mean for you? Define each of the "best practices" or duties above with bullet points or short sentences.

Step Four: Now once again consider each of the duties in this model, as you've defined them. For each, answer the following questions:

♦ How are people in our organization (or team) overall doing when it comes to this approach to good citizenship? What can we do to get better?

◆ How are you doing as an individual when it comes to this approach? What can you do to get better?

Step Five: HOMEWORK. Consider bringing this model forward with you into your day-to-day work. Try to be a better citizen, according to this model. Keep track of how you are doing in writing. Talk about it with your manager in your one-on-ones.

Good Citizenship: Lesson Plan #7 – The "Solid Standards" Model

Step One: Consider the following model of "good citizenship."

"Solid standards":

- Be on time, or a little bit early.
- Don't take long breaks.
- Don't leave early, and even stay a little late sometimes.
- Under-promise and over-deliver.
- Don't badmouth others and try not to speak of others unless they are present.
- Keep your word.
- Keep confidences.
- Be an accurate source of information.
- Don't keep other people waiting.
- Overdress, rather than underdress.
- Practice old-fashioned good manners; for example, saying "please," "thank you," "you're welcome," "excuse me," "I'm sorry," and if appropriate, addressing people by Mr., Ms., Doctor, Professor, and so on.

Step Two: What do you think of this model?

Brainstorm: Why might this approach to citizenship be in the best interests of the organization? Why might this approach to citizenship be in your best interests as an employee? What are the downsides?

Step Three: Consider each of the "best practices" or duties in this model, one by one. For each, answer the following questions: Can you think of examples of individuals exemplifying good citizenship in this way? What would it mean for you? Define each of the "best practices" or duties above with bullet points or short sentences.

Step Four: Now once again consider each of the duties in this model, as you've defined them. For each, answer the following questions:

- How are people in our organization (or team) overall doing when it comes to this approach to good citizenship? What can we do to get better?
- How are you doing as an individual when it comes to this approach? What can you do to get better?

Step Five: HOMEWORK. Consider bringing this model forward with you into your day-to-day work. Try to be a better citizen, according to this model. Keep track of how you are doing in writing. Talk about it with your manager in your one-on-ones.

Good Citizenship: Lesson Plan #8 – The "Personal Sacrifice" Model

Step One: Consider the following model of "good citizenship." Personal sacrifices:

- Giving your employer the benefit of a doubt when explanations are not immediately forthcoming
- Patience in the face of protracted difficulties or delayed rewards
- Candor and cooperation with peers and managers
- Offering your employer first rights of refusal in the face of a seemingly better offer
- Doing more than you are required to do and expending discretionary effort in your work
- Arriving early, staying late, working through breaks, coming to work without notice at the last minute, and chipping in to perform additional work outside your "job description" in order to cover for someone else coming up short

Step Two: What do you think of this model?

Brainstorm: Why might this approach to citizenship be in the best interests of the organization? Why might this approach to citizenship be in your best interests as an employee? What are the downsides?

Step Three: Consider each of the "best practices" or duties in this model, one by one. For each, answer the following questions: Can you think of examples of individuals exemplifying good citizenship in this way? What would it mean for you? Define each of the "best practices" or duties above with bullet points or short sentences.

Step Four: Now once again consider each of the duties in this model, as you've defined them. For each, answer the following questions:

- How are people in our organization (or team) overall doing when it comes to this approach to good citizenship? What can we do to get better?
- How are you doing as an individual when it comes to this approach? What can you do to get better?

Step Five: HOMEWORK. Consider bringing this model forward with you into your day-to-day work. Try to be a better citizen, according to this model. Keep track of how you are doing in writing. Talk about it with your manager in your one-on-ones.

Good Citizenship: Lesson Plan #9 – The Theodore Roosevelt Model

Step One: Consider the following very simple model of "good citizenship":

> Theodore Roosevelt, the twenty-sixth president of the United States, defined good citizenship for an individual as being "able and willing to pull his weight."

Step Two: What do you think of this model?

Brainstorm: Why might this approach to citizenship be in the best interests of the organization? Why might this approach to citizenship be in your best interests as an employee? Are there good reasons to reject this approach to citizenship?

Step Three: Consider this model of good citizenship. Can you think of examples of individuals exemplifying good citizenship in this way? What would it mean for you to accept, embrace, and observe this approach to good citizenship?

Step Four: Now consider:

◆ How are people in our organization (or team) overall doing when it comes to this approach to good citizenship? What can we do to get better?

◆ How are you doing as an individual when it comes to this approach? What can you do to get better?

Step Five: HOMEWORK. Consider bringing this model forward with you into your day-to-day work. Try to be a better citizen, according to this model. Keep track of how you are doing in writing. Talk about it with your manager in your one-on-ones.

Good Citizenship: Lesson Plan #10 – Create Your Own Model

Step One: Create your own model of "good citizenship." Rules based? Values based? Process based? Outcome based? What is the basis of your model and how would others know if they saw it? How to emulate it?

Step Two: Make the case for your model.

Brainstorm: Why might this approach to citizenship be in the best interests of the organization? Why might this approach to citizenship be in your best interests as an employee? What are the downsides?

Step Three: Consider each of the "best practices" or duties in this model, one by one. For each, answer the following questions: Can you think of examples of individuals exemplifying good citizenship in this way? What would it mean for you? Define each of the "best practices" or duties above with bullet points or short sentences.

Step Four: Now once again consider each of the duties in this model, as you've defined them. For each, answer the following questions:

- How are people in our organization (or team) overall doing when it comes to this approach to good citizenship? What can we do to get better?
- How are you doing as an individual when it comes to this approach? What can you do to get better?

Step Five: HOMEWORK. Consider bringing this model forward with you into your day-to-day work. Try to be a better citizen, according to this model. Keep track of how you are doing in writing. Talk about it with your manager in your one-on-ones.

Teaching Service

Service: Approaching relationships in terms of what you have to offer – respect, commitment, hard work, creativity, sacrifice – rather than what you need or want.

BRIDGING THE GAP

What is so special about the old-fashioned idea of service?

On a strictly rational basis, service is just another spin on the transactional logic of employment, like any market-based relationship: you get what you pay for. That notion of "service" is reciprocal, quid pro quo, each side of the value proposition.

Yet, somehow, like citizenship, the concept of service implies more. There is a yearning desire on the part of many older, more experienced people for a demonstration of something deeper – a kind of selflessness. When people talk about the missing values of "service" as a mindset, there is almost a religious or moralistic implication. Somehow, the spirit of generosity and the act of giving is supposed to have its own hidden long-term benefits to the generous giver. Maybe it is just a more cosmic sense of the quid pro quo – like Karma. What goes around comes around.

Whether or not this is true on some cosmic level, it is a very hard case to make to today's workforce, unless you happen to be their spiritual adviser. Nonetheless, experience does show that when you give people a taste of selfless giving, it can be so nourishing that it creates its own self-reinforcing virtuous cycle.

In any case, whatever philosophical or logical underpinning one chooses, this deep sense of "service" for its own sake is in great demand and short supply.

It is easy to understand why this might be a very desirable mindset, especially in your employees. I remember a senior partner at the law firm where I was an associate in the early 1990s said to me, "You should be prepared to jump in front of a bus for this firm." I said to myself, "For G-d? Yes. For my family? Yes. For my country? Yes. For this firm? I don't think so."

Ask yourself: If you want to ask your employees to give of themselves with a level of selflessness – service for its own sake – then what exactly are you asking them to serve?

- Is it the organization?
- The leadership?
- You, the manager?
- Their coworkers?
- The customers?
- The mission?

The most obvious answer is "mission." Mission-driven work draws people in particular who want to serve others by giving of themselves. The military is a common example; serving in the military is dangerous and doesn't pay well, but it gives young people the chance to help keep their country strong and their fellow citizens safe. Charitable work: Feeding the hungry or building houses for the poor. Health care: Healing the sick is definitely mission-driven work! Mission-driven work is instructive precisely because it draws those who are more inclined to feel that "something beyond" motivation that looks like old-fashioned loyalty.

I was struck by this comment from a very experienced leader in a large hospital: "In health care, we have always attracted people based on our healing mission. That's still true today for most of the young people. The healing mission brings them in the door. But as soon as they walk through the door, they want to know how this job compares to other jobs they could get doing the same mission: What's the pay? What are the hours? How are the people? What are the work conditions? Etc. In other words: It's the mission, plus, plus, plus."

I've heard this from so many leaders in mission-driven organizations. No matter how committed they may be to the mission, when mission-driven work is also the source of their livelihood, employees usually care a lot about making sure the transactional elements of the job are also fair and square. That's especially true if there are multiple employers for whom the employee might pursue the same or a similar mission. Even in the military (where you can't exactly go work for the competition), you can choose the Army, the Navy, the Air Force, the Marines, the Coast Guard, or maybe you can pursue a similar mission in national security, intelligence work, law enforcement, public safety, rescue, diplomacy, the Peace Corps, or whatever. In a free market for labor, even mission-driven employees are usually going to make their career choices based on mission, plus, plus, plus.

Of course, every employer has a mission of one sort of another. Some missions are more charitable than others. If your organization's mission is to sell a middle-price-range casual dining experience, that is a perfectly valid mission well worth pursuing! And I thank you on behalf of all of us who enjoy your meals. But let's agree that this is not exactly a "charitable" mission. No doubt a big part of what the owners are trying to do is make money. Can you blame them? So how can they blame their employees – of any age – for asking: "What's in it for me?"

Remember: If you can introduce your employees to the concept of service for its own sake and start to give them a taste of selfless giving, this can be such a nourishing experience that it creates its own self-reinforcing virtuous cycle.

Here's why employees should care about developing a service mindset.

Yes, you are getting paid and you reap the rewards and benefits of being an employee in this organization. So, yes, the organization is your customer. The leadership is your customer. Your manager is your customer. The customers are your customers. Your colleagues here are your customers. Even our partners and vendors are your customers. In relation to you, in this job, everyone is your customer. In this scenario, you are the only one who is not the customer.

But there is much more to the service mindset than just the other side of your paycheck! The truth that everybody knows but nobody likes to acknowledge is that one super high-performing employee is worth more on some deep level – and is valued so much more by everyone – than three or four mediocre employees.

If you are one of those high-performing employees, you already know that. If you are not one of those high-performing employees, you should learn that and become one! Where do you begin?

At the very least, you need to know the bare minimum requirements and the gold standard of performance, the cardinal rules of conduct, and the outer limits of your discretion. In every working relationship with every person at every level, make sure you understand not only how to meet the basic expectations of the job, but how to go above and beyond those expectations. If you fail to meet a commitment, be honest and forthright about it. If you make a commitment, deliver on that commitment.

If you don't get the extra rewards you hope for – or deserve – right away, be patient. Be understanding. After all, doing a great job and delivering on your commitments is what you were hired to do in the first place. That's why you get paid and you get to keep working here. If you don't benefit immediately from bending over backward and jumping through hoops, then write off the short-term loss as a cost of doing business, an investment in the bank account of your reputation at work. Or maybe a long-term deposit in your karmic "service" account.

Build a reputation, not only for doing great work every day, all day long, ahead of schedule, under budget, and with a big smile on your face. Once you deliver on that part of the deal consistently for some period of time, you put yourself in a position to seize opportunities to go above and beyond. When they present themselves, focus like a laser beam on the value you bring to the table. What hard work can you offer? What extra efforts can you make? What value can you add? Look out for really tough assignments, special assignments, and roles that are hard to fill. Look for ways you can sacrifice to save your boss, your colleagues, your direct reports, and anyone and everyone else time, energy, resources, and trouble. Sometimes, the best thing you can do is sacrifice, suffer, and give, give, give, and give until it hurts.

Don't be annoyed when all the pressure is on you. Instead, be grateful. This is your big chance to prove yourself and make a huge investment in your growing reputation for service.

Service: Lesson Plan #1 – Introduction

Step One: *Brainstorm*: What does "service" mean to you?

Step Two: Consider the following definition of "service": "Approaching relationships in terms of what you have to offer – respect, commitment, hard work, creativity, sacrifice – rather than what you need or want."

Brainstorm: Why is this approach to service in the best interests of the organization? Why is this approach to service in your best interests as an employee?

Step Three: Consider the following dimensions of service. For each one: Why is this an important component of service?

- Offering respect
- Offering commitment
- Offering hard work
- Offering creativity
- Offering sacrifice

Step Four: Consider the following dimensions of service. For each one: Can you think of examples of individuals exemplifying this dimension? Can you describe the example in detail? What happened? Where? When? Who was involved?

- Offering respect
- Offering commitment
- Offering hard work
- Offering creativity
- Offering sacrifice

Step Five: Consider the following dimensions of service. For each one: Can you think of examples of a time when you exemplified this dimension – inside or outside of work? Can you describe the example in detail? What happened? Where? When? Who else was involved?

- Offering respect
- Offering commitment
- Offering hard work
- Offering creativity
- Offering sacrifice

Step Six: Now consider the following dimensions of service. For each one: Define each one with bullet points or short sentences.

- Offering respect
- Offering commitment
- Offering hard work
- Offering creativity
- Offering sacrifice

Step Seven: Consider the following dimensions of service. For each one: How are you doing personally when it comes to this dimension of service? Are you performing at 100%? If not, then what percentage would you give your performance? Where is the gap? What do you need to do to improve?

- Offering respect
- Offering commitment
- Offering hard work
- Offering creativity
- Offering sacrifice

Service: Lesson Plan #2 – Common Myths About "Service" in the Workplace

Consider the following myths about the nature of "service" in the workplace, one by one. For each one: Why is this statement a myth? Have you ever seen this myth in action? Can you describe the example in detail? What happened? Where? When? Who was involved? What lessons do you draw from this example?

> **Myth #1:** If you are a high performer, then your boss shouldn't tell you how to do your job.
>
> **Myth #2:** In order to be creative at work, you need to be left alone to do things your own way.
>
> **Myth #3:** If someone else is getting special treatment, then you should too.
>
> **Myth #4:** The path to success is catering to your boss's style and preferences.
>
> **Myth #5:** "Making friends" with your boss is smart workplace politics.
>
> **Myth #6:** Hiding from mistakes and problems is a good way to avoid trouble.
>
> **Myth #7:** No news is good news, but being "coached" on your performance is bad news.
>
> **Myth #8:** If your boss doesn't like to read paperwork, you don't need to keep track of your performance in writing.
>
> **Myth #9:** If you are not a "people person," then you'll have a hard time getting ahead in the workplace.
>
> **Myth #10:** Some bosses are just too busy to meet with you.

Service: Lesson Plan #3 – Realities About Service in the Workplace

Consider the following realities about the nature of "service" in the workplace, one by one. For each one: Why is this statement a reality? Have you ever seen this reality in action? Can you describe the example in detail? What happened? Where? When? Who was involved? What lessons do you draw from this example?

Reality: No matter how good you may be at your job, everybody needs guidance, direction, and support in order to succeed.

Reality: If you really want to be creative at work, the first thing you need to know is exactly what is and what is not up to you.

Reality: The reality is that we are not all winners, as everybody knows. Treating everybody the same, regardless of their performance, is totally unfair.

Reality: Your best path to success is making sure you have a regular structured dialogue where you get the guidance, direction, support, and coaching you need.

Reality: The smartest workplace politics is to keep your work relationships focused on the work.

Reality: When you deal with mistakes and problems as they occur, you are much more likely to solve them while they are still small and manageable, before they get out of control.

Reality: Being coached on your performance is an opportunity to improve – and that is always good news.

Reality: You owe it to yourself and the organization to keep track of everything you do in writing.

Reality: Whether or not you are a "people person," learn and practice the "service" mindset and you will be everybody's "go to" person.

Reality: No matter how busy your boss may be, your boss does not have time not to meet with you on a regular basis.

Service: Lesson Plan #4 – Myths Versus Realities in the Workplace

Consider the following myth versus reality pairs along with the explanations "why?" For each one: Have you seen examples of this in the real world? Can you describe the example in detail? What happened? Where? When? Who was involved? What lessons do you draw from this example?

> **Myth #1:** If you are a high performer, then your boss shouldn't tell you how to do your job.
> VERSUS
> **Reality:** No matter how good you may be at your job, everybody needs guidance, direction, and support in order to succeed.

WHY? You need to make sure your work fits with your overall company's mission. You need to have articulated goals and the guidelines and parameters for your tasks and responsibilities spelled out. You need to be given concrete deadlines, clear timelines, and reasonable performance benchmarks to meet. And your boss is the person who needs to communicate these requirements to you and to make sure you stay on track. That's the only way to become and remain a high performer. But if you are a high performer, you probably already know all that.

> **Myth #2:** In order to be creative at work, you need to be left alone to do things your own way.
> VERSUS
> **Reality:** If you really want to be creative at work, the first thing you need to know is exactly what is and what is not up to you.

WHY? So much of what gets done at work is simply not up to you. You need to know the requirements of every task, responsibility, or project before you can even think about being creative. Even if you are in a creative position, only when you know what is actually up to you can you uncover the small space where you can be creative.

Myth #3: If someone else is getting special treatment, then you should too.
VERSUS

Reality: The reality is that we are not all winners, as everybody knows. Treating everybody the same, regardless of their performance, is totally unfair.

WHY? If someone else is getting special treatment, then figure out exactly what that person did to earn the special treatment and what exactly you need to do to earn the special treatment you want. Why would it be fair to treat everybody in a workplace exactly the same? That's only fair in a commune. If your coworkers are receiving rewards that you are not getting, take that as a big reality check. What you need is a fair and accurate assessment of your performance so that you can continually improve and thereby earn more of the rewards you want. Don't be the squeaky wheel asking for more. Be the self-starting high performer who is constantly earning more.

Myth #4: The path to success is catering to your boss's style and preferences.
VERSUS

Reality: Your best path to success is making sure you have a regular structured dialogue where you get the guidance, direction, support, and coaching you need.

WHY? It is true that you need to align yourself as best you can with what "works" for each of your bosses. Some bosses prefer updates in writing; others prefer verbal reports. Some bosses prefer big-picture reports. Others like to keep track of the details. You should certainly try to tune in to each boss's preferences, but you cannot afford to compromise the basic elements you need in order to succeed: clear, realistic expectations every step of the way; the necessary resources to complete your tasks; fair, accurate, and honest feedback; and appropriate recognition and rewards for your work.

Myth #5: "Making friends" with your boss is smart workplace politics.
VERSUS

Reality: The smartest workplace politics is to keep your work relationships focused on the work.

WHY? False friendships are a waste of time and real friendships may be wonderful in your personal life, but they are likely to complicate your situation at work. That is not to say that real friendships do not or should not occur in the workplace. Of course they do. Real friendships develop over time at work, including friendships with people who are your boss. If that's your situation, then you'll have to work hard to protect that friendship from the realities of the workplace. What is the best workplace politics? Build authentic relationships with your bosses by developing genuine rapport by talking about the work.

Myth #6: Hiding from mistakes and problems is a good way to avoid trouble.
VERSUS
Reality: When you deal with mistakes and problems as they occur, you are much more likely to solve them while they are still small and manageable, before they get out of control.

WHY? When you gloss over small mistakes without solving them, sometimes they drift away – but they are likely to recur. Small problems that recur incessantly cause difficult confrontations when coworkers or the boss finally explodes in an outburst of frustration. Other times those recurring small problems become part of the fabric of your work. But sometimes small mistakes and problems fester and grow and, over time, become big problems. Solving a problem after it has festered is much more difficult than preventing that problem in the first place, or solving it while it was smaller. Plus, in the midst of a problem, neither you nor the boss in question is going to be at your best. By then, everybody is stressed, frustrated, and in a hurry. If you include regular problem solving in your ongoing one-on-one dialogue with every single boss, then nine out of ten performance problems will be solved quickly and easily or will be avoided altogether.

Myth #7: No news is good news, but being "coached" on your performance is bad news.
VERSUS

Reality: Being coached on your performance is an opportunity to improve – and that is always good news.

WHY? Good coaching is the constant banter of focus, improvement, and accountability: "What can I teach you right now? What can you improve right now?" A great coach helps you remember to be purposeful about every single detail to build your skills. From focusing, you learn focus itself. Look for the real teachers among your bosses and soak up their teachings. Assure the boss that you very much welcome candid feedback in detail, both positive and corrective. Try to turn every one-on-one conversation with your boss into a coaching session:

Myth #8: If your boss doesn't like to read paperwork, you don't need to keep track of your performance in writing.
VERSUS
Reality: You owe it to yourself and the organization to keep track of everything you do in writing.

WHY? Most managers monitor employee performance only incidentally, when they happen to observe the employee working; if they are presented with the employee's work product; if there is a big win; or if there is a notable problem. They rarely document employee performance unless they are required to do so, leaving no written track record other than those bottom-line reports that tell so little about the day-to-day actions of each employee. Whether or not your boss keeps track of your day-to-day performance in writing, you should.

Myth #9: If you are not a "people person," then you'll have a hard time getting ahead in the workplace.
VERSUS
Reality: Whether or not you are a "people person," learn and practice the "service" mindset and you will be everybody's "go to" person.

WHY? Some people are unusually charismatic, observant, receptive, quick-witted, articulate, engaging, energetic, and likeable. That does not get you anywhere near as far as being the person who is always focused on what you have to offer.

> **Myth #10:** Some bosses are just too busy to meet with you.
> VERSUS
> **Reality:** No matter how busy your boss may be, your boss does not have time *not* to meet with you on a regular basis.

WHY? When your boss doesn't spend time one-on-one with you, things go wrong – sometimes very wrong. That's because expectations often remain unclear, misunderstandings occur, you don't get the resources you need, you don't receive regular feedback to guide you, and even if you succeed against all odds, you probably won't get the credit you deserve. If you push your boss to put the management time where it belongs – up front before anything goes right, wrong, or average – things will go much better. If you make sure the time every boss spends with you is effective and pays off in productivity, bosses are going to want to give you that time. You will gain a reputation for making good use of management time.

Service: Lesson Plan #5 – The "Be a Great Employee" Model of Service

Step One: Consider the following vision of the service mindset in the workplace.

Be the employee who says to every boss, "Great news, I'm going to make a commitment to serve! I'm going to help you by getting a bunch of work done very well, very fast, all day long. I'm going to work with you to make sure I understand exactly what you expect of me. On every task, I'm going to break big deadlines into smaller, concrete performance benchmarks. I'm going to learn standard operating procedures and use checklists. I'm going to keep track of everything I'm doing and exactly how I'm doing it. I'm going to help you monitor, measure, and document my performance every step of the way. I'm going to solve problems as soon as they occur and, if I come to you for your help, you'll know I really need you. I'm going to learn and grow and be able to take on more and more responsibility. Count on me. With your help, I'm going to be really valuable to you!"

Step Two: *Brainstorm*: Can you think of examples of individuals exemplifying this? Can you describe the example in detail? What happened? Where? When? Who was involved?

Step Three: *Brainstorm*: Can you think of examples of a time when you exemplified this? Can you describe the example in detail? What happened? Where? When? Who else was involved?

Step Four: *Brainstorm*: How are you doing personally when it comes to this dimension of service? Are you performing at 100%? If not, then what percentage would you give your performance? Where is the gap? What do you need to do to improve?

Service: Lesson Plan #6 – The "Service" Approach to One-on-Ones Between Managers and Direct Reports

Step One: Consider: The key to figuring out what your manager needs from you is to build a regular one-on-one dialogue with every manager to whom you report.

Brainstorm: What would it look like for you to do that? How many managers do you report to now? Who are they? Consider each of them, one by one. For each one, ask yourself: How often do you think you should meet with this manager? When would be the best time to meet? Where? How long? What should you discuss? How can you prepare? What would it take to start scheduling those one-on-ones on a regular basis?

Step Two: Following is a list of the "four basics" that every person must get from their manager in order to be able to succeed. Consider each of the managers to whom you report, one by one. For each one: Do you get all four of the basics on a regular basis? Where is the gap? What would it take to improve? What can you do to improve the situation?

The four basics that you absolutely must take responsibility for getting in your ongoing dialogue with your boss:

1. Clearly spelled out and reasonable expectations, including specific guidelines and a concrete timetable.
2. The skills, tools, and resources necessary to meet those expectations or else an acknowledgment that you are being asked to meet those expectations without them.
3. Accurate and honest feedback about your performance as well as course-correcting direction when necessary.
4. The fair quid pro quo – recognition and rewards – in exchange for your performance.

Step Three: Consider: How often you should meet with your boss or bosses depends partly on the nature of the work you are engaged in with each of them. How often you should meet with a particular manager will also be determined by their particular style and preferences and also by what works for you. In an ideal world, maybe YOU would talk with every single boss – reviewing your work and getting set up for success that day – every single day.

Brainstorm:

- ◆ How are people in our organization (or team) overall doing when it comes to this approach? What can we do to get better?
- ◆ How are you doing as an individual when it comes to this approach? What can you do to get better?
- ◆ For each of your managers: How often do you need to meet? Where is the gap? What would it take to improve? What can you do to improve the situation?

Step Four: Consider: With each boss, you will have to decide what to focus on and discuss at each one-on-one. Before your meetings, you should ask yourself the following: Are there problems that haven't been spotted yet? Problems that need to be solved? Resources that need to be obtained? Are there any instructions or goals that are not clear? Has anything happened since we last talked that the boss should know about? Are there questions that need to be answered by your boss? At the very least, in these one-one-ones, you need to receive updates on your progress. Get input from your boss while you have the chance. And think about what input you should be providing to the boss based on what you are learning on the front line. Strategize together. Try to get a little advice, support, motivation, and, yes, even inspiration once in a while.

Brainstorm:

- ◆ How are people in our organization (or team) overall doing when it comes to this approach? What can we do to get better?
- ◆ How are you doing as an individual when it comes to this approach? What can you do to get better?
- ◆ For each of your managers: What do you need to be discussing? Where is the gap? What would it take to improve? What can you do to improve the situation?

Step Five: HOMEWORK. Take the initiative. Schedule regular one-on-one management meetings with every single manager to whom you report. Make your one-on-one time with every boss brief, straightforward, efficient, and all about the work. But make sure you get that regular one-on-one time with every boss you answer to directly at any given time. Be sure to get the four basics listed in step two.

Service: Lesson Plan #7 – The Service Approach to Meeting Attendance and Participation

Step One: Consider the following vision of the service approach to your attendance and participation in meetings:

◆ Meetings serve their purpose. They are ideal for sharing information with the whole group and are often necessary to bring people that working interdependently together to hear about what everyone is doing, what issues are coming up in their projects, and so on. Inevitably, you will attend more than your share of team meetings. How can you make the most of them?

◆ Before attending any meeting or presentation, make sure you know what the meeting is about and whether your attendance is required or requested. Identify what your role in the meeting is: What information are you responsible for communicating or gathering? Prepare in advance: Is there any material you should review or read before the meeting? Are there any conversations you need to have before the meeting? If you are making a presentation, prepare even more. Ask yourself exactly what value you have to offer the group. If you are not a primary actor in the meeting, often the best thing you can do is say as little as possible and practice good meeting manners. If you are tempted to speak up, ask yourself: Is this a point that everyone needs to hear, right here and now? If you have a question, could it be asked at a later time, off-line? Remember some meetings are often a waste of time. In those meetings, try not to say a single word that will unnecessarily lengthen it.

Step Two: *Brainstorm:*

◆ How are people in our organization (or team) overall doing when it comes to this approach? What can we do to get better?

◆ Can you think of examples of individuals exemplifying this? Can you describe the example in detail? What happened? Where? When? Who was involved?

◆ Can you think of examples of a time when you exemplified this? Can you describe the example in detail? What happened? Where? When? Who else was involved?

◆ How are you doing as an individual when it comes to this approach? What can you do to get better?

Service: Lesson Plan #8 – Helping Your Boss Monitor Your Performance

Step One: Consider the following best practices for helping your boss monitor your performance:

◆ *Provide drafts or samples of your work in progress on a regular basis.* If you want to make sure the work you are doing meets your boss's requirements, don't wait until a routine review of the work comes along; by then you might discover you've been doing a task the wrong way for quite some time. Even if you have a clear deliverable with a concrete deadline, don't wait until you deliver the final product to find out if the deliverable meets the expectations. Instead, check with your boss early on to make sure that you are going in the right direction. That means actually showing the boss drafts or samples of what you are doing, not just describing it. Say, "This is an example of the product I am building. Does this meet your requirements? What adjustments do I need to make?" You are much better off having that conversation early and often so that by the time the deadline rolls around for the final deliverable, there will be no surprises.

◆ *Any opportunities you can seize to help your boss spot-check your work will help you identify and solve any hidden problems.* For example, if you manage a database, ask your boss to walk through some records at random with you to spot-check them for quality. If you write reports, ask your boss to look at early drafts or draft sections. If you make phone calls, ask your boss if you can record them and listen to a random sample together so he can help you improve. If you make widgets, ask your boss to look at some half-done widgets with you to see how they are coming along.

◆ *Ask your boss to watch you work.* If you want to make absolutely sure that you are accomplishing a task the way your boss wants you to do it – especially if you are not responsible for producing a tangible end product – one of the most effective ways to get that clarity is to ask the manager to watch you work. Watching you complete a task will give them a clear view of what you are doing and how you are doing it. For example, if you are in a customer service role, having your boss watch you interact with a customer will reveal more about your customer service performance than any batch of customer feedback surveys. In particular, if you are having difficulty succeeding with a specific task, ask your boss to "shadow" you while you accomplish the task. If your boss is really good at the task, they are likely to have some good advice for doing it better.

♦ *Give your boss an account of your performance.* In every one-on-one conversation with every boss, you should be providing a full and honest account of exactly what you've done on your assignments for that boss since your last conversation: "These are the concrete actions I've taken. This is what I did and how I did it. These are the steps I followed in order to meet or exceed the expectations we set together." Once you've given a full and honest account, you and your boss will be better able to clarify next steps. As long as you are engaged in an ongoing, consistent one-on-one dialogue with that boss, this element of helping your boss monitor your performance will become routine.

♦ *Use self-monitoring tools.* Help your boss keep track of your concrete actions by making good, rigorous use of self-monitoring tools like project plans, checklists, and activity logs. Monitor in writing whether you are meeting the goals and deadlines laid out in a project plan. Make notes and use checklists, and report to your boss at regular intervals. Use an activity log, a diary noting contemporaneously exactly what you are doing all day, including breaks and interruptions. Each time you move on to a new activity, note the time and the new activity you are turning to.

♦ *Spread the word.* Ask customers, vendors, coworkers, and everyone else you work with to give you honest feedback about your performance in relation to them. Ask them, in writing, "How am I doing?" Consider passing their responses on to your boss. Remember, one of the most consistent sources of information most bosses have about the work of their employees is hearsay. People talk. Word spreads. You should know what people think about your work and use that data as feedback to help you improve. But this feedback will also be important to pass on to your boss so that you have some input in the general hearsay about your work.

Step Two: Take them one at a time. *Brainstorm.* For each one:

- How are people in our organization (or team) overall doing when it comes to this approach? What can we do to get better?
- Can you think of examples of individuals exemplifying this? Can you describe the example in detail? What happened? Where? When? Who was involved?
- Can you think of examples of a time when you exemplified this? Can you describe the example in detail? What happened? Where? When? Who else was involved?
- How are you doing as an individual when it comes to this approach? What can you do to get better?

Service: Lesson Plan #9 – Putting Yourself on a Performance Improvement Plan

Step One: Consider the following:

Put yourself on a PIP – Performance Improvement Plan. In many organizations, PIPs have a bad name. So call it something else if you like. How about a "Continuous Improvement Plan"? Whatever you call it, this is the perfect format for helping your boss document your performance every step of the way: Together with your boss, spell out expectations for your performance in terms of concrete actions that you can control. Keep track in writing as you complete each to-do item and meet each requirement, as you achieve each goal and beat each deadline. Regularly report to your boss exactly how and when your concrete actions met or exceeded the expectations you set together. Help your boss document exactly how and when your concrete actions meet expectations every step of the way.

Step Two: *Brainstorm*:

- What do you think about this approach?
- What would be the benefits to you? What about to your boss? What about to the organization?
- What would be the burdens?

Teaching How to Play Your Position

Playing your position: Doing the part assigned (or relegated) to you to support the larger mission; coordinating, cooperating, and collaborating with others in pursuit of a shared goal; supporting and celebrating the success of others.

BRIDGING THE GAP

Many of our clients have been experimenting with strategies to create a greater sense of belonging and teamwork, through peer networking and peer bonding.

- Some employers have tried to facilitate peer bonding by creating so-called "self-managed teams." It turns out there is no such thing as a "self-managed team": somebody always takes charge, sometimes the right person and sometimes a ringleader who causes trouble.
- Other organizations have tried to implement "best friend at work" programs, where they try to help employees form friendships with colleagues. Most young people either shrug or cringe at these "best friend" programs.
- Some organizations encourage employees to form affinity groups around shared interests, activities, or even causes. These tend to be more or less harmless, unless they become a way to affirm cliques; usually they are only slight distractions at work, although distractions nonetheless.
- Some organizations promote socializing among colleagues through meals, happy hours, events, and parties. Most people of any age can appreciate employer-sponsored events or meals or beverages, unless they become another way to affirm cliques, or lead to selective exclusion. After-work socializing inevitably excludes those who just want to get home after work . . . or to the gym. . . or to walk the dog . . . or whatever. And often those young employees who appreciate the after-work partying the very most find themselves embarrassed in front of their colleagues (and sometimes even on their way out of a job) as a result of some major "social" misstep.

Our research shows consistently that people are least likely to form significant lasting peer bonds in workplaces with less challenging work, less structure, less supervision, and less interaction with authority figures. The greater the challenge, structure, supervision, and interaction with authority figures, the more likely people – of all ages – are to form significant peer bonds in the workplace. Yes, the key to creating those so-important authentic personal "loyalties" among employees is creating conditions in which they can do lots of challenging work together under the strong direction of a highly engaged leader.

I always point to examples from the military, especially when it comes to peer bonding and teamwork. When young soldiers, airmen, marines, and sailors talk about their "loyalty," they invoke first and foremost their commitment to each other – to their peers and to their most immediate leaders. But those peer bonds are hardly forming organically. They are not "self-managed," but rather have a strict chain of command with clear leaders who are strong and highly engaged. They don't get to choose who is going to be on their team. They don't get to choose their own peer leaders. They don't get to choose their own mission. They don't get to choose their own positions on the team. Not everybody gets to be the MVP. Not everybody gets a trophy. The peer bonding is not forced, but all of the conditions are forced and the peer bonding follows.

Of course, the military has a rare combination of profound patriotic mission, life-threatening gravity, and extraordinary resources. Those are hard conditions to approximate for most leaders in most workplaces. Still, you can be very thankful that lives are not on the line. And you can still draw many great lessons about building the conditions to support great teamwork. The strongest relationships among people in the workplace form in environments with a strong focus on the shared mission, the shared work, and the common ground. Yes, it is important to value and leverage everybody's different strengths on a team. But the key to supporting the spirit of "teamwork" per se is focusing on what everybody has in common: nobody on the team chose the team or the mission or the positions or the leaders. But everybody on the team did choose to be in this job at this time. As long as they remain here, they are in this together. They must depend upon each other in order to succeed. So they must each be dependable to each other.

Yes, your best employees can see that they pull more weight than the weaker members of the team. Sometimes they have to be reminded that, no matter how much weight they carry on their own, they are not doing their job 100% unless they are also helping their other team members succeed.

Here's why employees should care about teamwork.

No matter where you work, no matter what you do, your work probably involves dealing with other people – internally and externally – here, there, and everywhere. Most likely you are forced to rely on the support and cooperation of many other people in the course of doing your own work every day. That means navigating a lot of interpersonal dynamics and a lot of dependency and interdependency. That's what a lot of people call "teamwork."

You've heard over and over again about the importance of good teamwork at work. Right?

For the most part, at work, you don't get to choose who is going to be on your team. You don't get to choose your own leaders. You don't get to choose your own mission. You don't get to choose your own position. Not everybody gets to be the MVP. Not everybody gets a trophy. But everybody on the team did choose to be in this job at this time. As long as you remain here, we are all in this together. We must depend upon each other in order to succeed. So we must each be dependable to each other.

Yes, some people pull more weight than others. Some people do more work, better, faster, and with a better attitude. But don't ever tell yourself you are doing a great job if you are not also being a great team player. Being a great team player is part of your job here. That means staying focused on our shared mission and how each person contributes to that shared mission. It means making yourself available and easy to work with. It means coordinating, cooperating, and collaborating with others. It means playing your assigned position as needed to support the larger effort. It means focusing on the best interest of the whole, sometimes at the expense of your own prominence. It means supporting your other team members, helping them succeed, and celebrating their successes.

In short, here's the bottom line: Some people really get things done. Right? And there are plenty of times when you need to get things done and you need someone's help. Right? So you want to be able to go to the right people, the ones who really get things done. Right? Those people are known as "go to" people. That's because everybody – just like you – wants to "go to" those people. Get it? "Go to" people don't just get things done. They get things done for other people. That's why "go to" people are the most in-demand people in the workplace. Because everyone knows they can be relied upon to deliver for the team. Be one!

Playing Your Position on the Team: Lesson Plan #1 – Introduction

Step One: *Brainstorm*: What does "playing your position on the team" mean to you?

Step Two: Consider the following definition of "teamwork": "Playing whatever role is needed to support the larger mission; coordinating, cooperating and collaborating with others in pursuit of a shared goal; supporting and celebrating the success of others."

Brainstorm: Why is this approach to teamwork in the best interests of the organization? Why is this approach to teamwork in your best interests as an employee?

Step Three: Consider the following dimensions of teamwork. For each one: Why is this an important component of teamwork? Teamwork:

- ♦ Playing whatever role is needed to support the larger mission
- ♦ Coordinating with others in pursuit of a shared goal
- ♦ Cooperating with others in pursuit of a shared goal
- ♦ Collaborating with others in pursuit of a shared goal
- ♦ Supporting the success of others
- ♦ Celebrating the success of others

Step Four: Consider the following dimensions of teamwork. For each one: Can you think of examples of individuals – inside or outside of work – exemplifying this dimension? Can you describe the example in detail? What happened? Where? When? Who was involved?

Teamwork:
- ♦ Playing whatever role is needed to support the larger mission
- ♦ Coordinating with others in pursuit of a shared goal
- ♦ Cooperating with others in pursuit of a shared goal
- ♦ Collaborating with others in pursuit of a shared goal
- ♦ Supporting the success of others
- ♦ Celebrating the success of others

Step Five: Consider the following dimensions of teamwork. For each one: Can you think of examples of a time when you exemplified this dimension – inside or outside of work? Can you describe the example in detail? What happened? Where? When? Who else was involved?

Teamwork:

- ◆ Playing whatever role is needed to support the larger mission
- ◆ Coordinating with others in pursuit of a shared goal
- ◆ Cooperating with others in pursuit of a shared goal
- ◆ Collaborating with others in pursuit of a shared goal
- ◆ Supporting the success of others
- ◆ Celebrating the success of others

Playing Your Position on the Team: Lesson Plan #2 – Defining the Dimensions of Playing Your Role on the Team/Teamwork

Step One: Consider the following dimensions of teamwork. For each one: Define each one. Break it down and spell it out with bullet points or short sentences.

Teamwork:

♦ Playing whatever role is needed to support the larger mission
♦ Coordinating with others in pursuit of a shared goal
♦ Cooperating with others in pursuit of a shared goal
♦ Collaborating with others in pursuit of a shared goal
♦ Supporting the success of others
♦ Celebrating the success of others

Step Two: Consider the following dimensions of teamwork. For each one: How are people in our organization (or team) overall doing when it comes to this approach? What can we do to get better?

Teamwork:

♦ Playing whatever role is needed to support the larger mission
♦ Coordinating with others in pursuit of a shared goal
♦ Cooperating with others in pursuit of a shared goal
♦ Collaborating with others in pursuit of a shared goal
♦ Supporting the success of others
♦ Celebrating the success of others

Step Three: Consider the following dimensions of teamwork. For each one: How are you doing personally when it comes to this dimension of service? Are you performing at 100%? If not, then what percentage would you give your performance? Where is the gap? What do you need to do to improve?

Teamwork:

♦ Playing whatever role is needed to support the larger mission
♦ Coordinating with others in pursuit of a shared goal

- Cooperating with others in pursuit of a shared goal
- Collaborating with others in pursuit of a shared goal
- Supporting the success of others
- Celebrating the success of others

Playing Your Position on the Team: Lesson Plan #3 – Your Role in Relation to the Mission

Step One: Consider the first dimension of being a great team player: Playing whatever role is needed to support the larger mission. *Brainstorm*:

- ◆ How would you describe the larger mission of this organization?
- ◆ How would you describe your role in relation to the mission?

Step Two: Drill down on your role. Make a list of all the different tasks, responsibilities, and projects that comprise your role. Now take them one by one. For each one: What do you actually do? How exactly does your work on that task, responsibility, or project contribute to the larger mission? Who relies upon you to do this work? What are the consequences if you don't deliver? What is the value added when you deliver successfully? How are you doing on this particular contribution to the mission? How can you improve?

Step Three: HOMEWORK. Discuss what you learned from this exercise with your manager in your next one-on-one.

Playing Your Position on the Team: Lesson Plan #4 – Coordinating, Cooperating, and Collaborating with Others

Step One: Consider the following dimensions of being a great team player:

♦ Coordinating with others in pursuit of a shared goal
♦ Cooperating with others in pursuit of a shared goal
♦ Collaborating with others in pursuit of a shared goal

Make a list of all the other people at work with whom you must coordinate, cooperate, and collaborate.

Step Two: Consider each of the people on your list, one by one. For each one:

♦ How would you describe that person's role in relation to the mission?
♦ For what do you need to rely upon that person at work?
  • On what work specifically do you coordinate, cooperate, and collaborate?
  • Where?
  • When?
  • How?
  • Who else is involved?
  • What happens?

How do you need this person to improve? What do you need this person to change so that you can get more of what you need/want?

Step Three: Consider each of the people on your list, again, one by one. For each one:

♦ How would you describe that person's role in relation to the mission?
♦ For what does that person need to rely upon you at work?

- On what work specifically do you coordinate, cooperate, and collaborate?
- Where?
- When?
- How?
- Who else is involved?
- What happens?

How do you need to improve? What do you need to change so this person can get more from you?

Step Four: HOMEWORK. Discuss what you learned from this exercise with your manager in your next one-on-one.

Playing Your Position on the Team: Lesson Plan #5 – Supporting and Celebrating the Success of Others

Step One: Consider the following dimensions of being a great team player:

- ◆ Supporting the success of others
- ◆ Celebrating the success of others

Make a list of all the people who should be supporting and celebrating your success at work. Presumably they are also people whose success you should be supporting and celebrating as well.

Step Two: Consider each of the people on your list, one by one. For each one:

- ◆ What does this person do to support your success? Can you think of examples?
- ◆ What does this person do to celebrate your success? Can you think of examples?

Step Three: Consider each of the people on your list, again, one by one. For each one:

- ◆ How would you describe that person's role in relation to the mission?
- ◆ What does success look like for this person in their role?
  - • What do you currently do to support this person's success?
  - • What else can you do? How can you improve?
  - • What do you currently do to celebrate this person's success?
  - • What else can you do? How can you improve?

Step Four: HOMEWORK. Discuss what you learned from this exercise with your manager in your next one-on-one.

Playing Your Position on the Team: Lesson Plan #6 – Identifying Your "Go To" People and Building Relationships with Them

Step One: What would it look like for you to actively develop "go to" people in all the key areas where you have recurring interdependency needs. "Go to" people are the people you know you can "go to" when you need something. They are people you can rely on. They are responsive. They are effective. They get things done.
Brainstorm:

◆ How do you identify "go to" people in all the right places?

◆ What cooperation and assistance do you anticipate needing from other colleagues – internal and external – to get your projects, tasks, and responsibilities done?

◆ Exactly who should you ask for what, when, and how?

◆ What is the precise nature of the working relationship with each person upon whom you may need to rely?

◆ What level of cooperation and assistance is appropriate and reasonable to request?

◆ In each case, is there more than one person to whom you could turn for cooperation and assistance? What should you do if they are having trouble getting cooperation and assistance from one person or another?

◆ What do you need to do to develop strong mutually supportive working relationships with these "go to" people?

Step Two: HOMEWORK. Discuss what you learned from this exercise with your manager in your next one-on-one.

Playing Your Position on the Team: Lesson Plan #7 – Becoming a "Go To" Person for Others

Step One: What would it look like for you to become a "go to" person yourself?
Brainstorm:

- ◆ How can you bend over backward to do things for other people?
- ◆ How can you become super-reliable?
- ◆ How can you become super-responsive?
- ◆ How can you become super-effective in getting things done?
- ◆ How can you make sure you always deliver on your commitments very well, very fast, all day long . . . especially for known "go to" people?
- ◆ How can you make sure to conduct yourself always in a professional manner with a great attitude?
- ◆ How can you develop a reputation as a "go to" person?

Step Two: *Brainstorm*: Can you think of examples of individuals exemplifying the "go to" person? Can you describe the example in detail? What happened? Where? When? Who was involved?

Step Three: *Brainstorm*: Can you think of examples of a time when you exemplified the "go to" person? Can you describe the example in detail? What happened? Where? When? Who else was involved?

Step Four: *Brainstorm*: How are you doing personally when it comes to becoming a "go to" person? Are you performing at 100%? If not, then what percentage would you give your performance? Where is the gap? What do you need to do to improve?

Step Five: HOMEWORK. Discuss what you learned from this exercise with your manager in your next one-on-one.

Playing Your Position on the Team: Lesson Plan #8 – How to Use Influence to Get Things Done

Step One: Consider how you can get better at gaining greater coordination, cooperation, and collaboration from others. Consider your options when it comes to the following strategies for using influence:

- *Build and draw on interpersonal influence.* Conduct yourself always in a businesslike professional manner. Be the person other people do not want to disappoint.
- *Use the influence of specific commitments.* Clear timelines for deliverables with reminders along the way are more likely to be fulfilled.
- *Seek to influence through persuasion.* Use good reasons to convince other people to deliver: "This is why you should do this for me. This is why it's a good thing for you, your team, and your company. This is why you should put my request first. This is why nothing else should get in the way."
- *Influence through facilitation.* Do everything possible to help support and assist other people in the fulfillment of their part. What are all the things you can do to make it easier for other people to deliver?

Step Two: Consider the preceding strategies, one by one. For each one: Have you seen examples of this in the real world? Can you describe the example in detail? What happened? Where? When? Who was involved? What lessons do you draw from this example?

Step Three: Consider these strategies again, one by one. For each one: How are you doing personally when it comes to using these strategies? Are you performing at 100%? If not, then what percentage would you give your performance? Where is the gap? What do you need to do to improve?

Step Four: HOMEWORK. Discuss what you learned from this exercise with your manager in your next one-on-one.

Playing Your Position on the Team: Lesson Plan #9 – Consider the Lessons About Teamwork from This US Air Force Special Operations Team

Step One: Consider the following story exemplifying great teamwork:

The young airman, one crew member among the 13-member crew of an important military aircraft, describes his role on the team's regular missions (which last as long as 10 hours): "My job is to lay face down in a window facing the ground in order to provide visual confirmation of the aircraft's electronic surveillance of the ground below. Basically I just lie down there with my eyes wide open and focused. We have very advanced systems on the plane, but I am the eyeballs. I need to provide visual [confirmation] to make sure we don't fire on any [friendly forces] or civilians. But I also am watching for muzzle flares which might indicate enemy forces. I also look for enemy fire directed at the plane. When we are fired on, we only have a few seconds to detect that and take countermeasures to protect the plane."

For hours at a time, this young airman stays focused and blinks as little as possible. During a 10-hour mission, there might only be a handful of incidents for which the airman would actually need to take notice and take action. Asked if it is hard to stay alert on the job, he says: "I don't have a choice. The difference between me giving 99% or 110% could be the difference between life or death for me, for people on the ground, and for my crew."

The crew numbered 13. Each person played a narrowly focused role and was critical to the safety and effective operation of the airplane and its mission. And every single one of them knew that they had no choice but to give 110% all the time, because the work of every single role is a life-or-death matter. For your sake, I hope that every move you make at work is not a life-or-death matter. Still, if you want to succeed, you would do well to follow this example of teamwork.

Step Two: *Brainstorm*:

- How would you describe this example of teamwork?
- What is admirable about this approach?
- What can we learn from this story?
- How are people in our organization (or team) overall doing when it comes to this level of teamwork? What can we do to get better?
- How are you doing as an individual when it comes to this approach? What can you do to get better?

Lesson Plan List:
92 Different Lesson Plans

Chapter 4: Teaching the Missing Basics of Professionalism

Self-Evaluation
Personal Responsibility
Attitude
Work Habits
Interpersonal Communication

- Self-Evaluation: Lesson Plan #1
- Self-Evaluation: Lesson Plan #2
  Evaluating Yourself on Ability, Skill, and Will
- Self-Evaluation: Lesson Plan #3
  Evaluating Yourself on Productivity, Quality, and Behavior
- Self-Evaluation: Lesson Plan #4
  Evaluating Yourself on the Key Soft Skills Competencies
- Self-Evaluation: Lesson Plan #5
  Drill Down on Understanding the Key Soft Skills Competencies
- Self-Evaluation: Lesson Plan #6
  Explore Your Own Successes with the Key Soft Skills
- Personal Responsibility: Lesson Plan #1
  Introduction
- Personal Responsibility: Lesson Plan #2
  All the Factors That Get in Your Way
- Personal Responsibility: Lesson Plan #3
  Considering the Most Common Factors, Mostly Outside Your Own Control, That Get in the Way at Work
- Personal Responsibility: Lesson Plan #4
  Response Power

- Positive Attitude: Lesson Plan #1
  Considering Theories of How to Be Your Best at Work
- Positive Attitude: Lesson Plan #2
  Defining "Good Attitude" Behaviors
- Positive Attitude: Lesson Plan #3
  Considering the Most Common Bad Attitudes
- Positive Attitude: Lesson Plan #4
  Considering Good Attitude Behaviors
- Positive Attitude: Lesson Plan #5
  For Individuals Who Need an Attitude Adjustment
- Good Work Habits: Lesson Plan #1
  Overview: Wellness, Self-Presentation, Timeliness, Productivity,
  Attention to Detail, Follow-Through, Initiative
- Good Work Habits: Lesson Plan #2
  Self-Assessment
- Good Work Habits: Lesson Plan #3
  Self-Improvement Planning
- Good Work Habits: Lesson Plan #4
  Wellness
- Good Work Habits: Lesson Plan #5
  Planning a Wellness Initiative
- Good Work Habits: Lesson Plan #6
  Self-Presentation
- Good Work Habits: Lesson Plan #7
  Using a Time Log to Learn to Start Living by a Schedule
- Good Work Habits: Lesson Plan #8
  How to Make a Basic Project Plan
- Good Work Habits: Lesson Plan #9
  Taking Notes and Making Checklists
- Good Work Habits: Lesson Plan #10
  How to Do a Time/Motion Study on Your Own Work
- Good Work Habits: Lesson Plan #11
  Spotlight on Follow-Through
- Good Work Habits: Lesson Plan #12
  Going the Extra Mile
- Interpersonal Communication Skills: Lesson Plan #1
  Introduction

- Interpersonal Communication Skills: Lesson Plan #2
  Self-Assessment
- Interpersonal Communication Skills: Lesson Plan #3
  Learning to Use the "People List"
- Interpersonal Communication Skills: Lesson Plan #4
  Put More Structure into Your Communication
- Interpersonal Communication Skills: Lesson Plan #5
  Put More Substance into Your Communication
- Interpersonal Communication Skills: Lesson Plan #6
  Preparing for Meetings
- Interpersonal Communication Skills: Lesson Plan #7
  Email Best Practices
- Interpersonal Communication Skills: Lesson Plan #8
  Communicating Remotely

Chapter 5: Teaching the Missing Basics of Critical Thinking

Proactive Learning
Problem Solving
Decision Making

- Proactive Learning: Lesson Plan #1
  Knowledge Work
- Proactive Learning: Lesson Plan #2
  Open Mind
- Proactive Learning: Lesson Plan #3
  Suspend Judgment, Question Assumptions, and Seek to Learn
- Proactive Learning: Lesson Plan #4
  Question Assumptions: What Do You Know? What Don't
  You Know?
- Proactive Learning: Lesson Plan #5
  Seeking Out Information, Technique, and Perspective
- Proactive Learning: Lesson Plan #6
  Studying Information to Build Knowledge
- Proactive Learning: Lesson Plan #7
  Practicing Technique to Build Skills
- Proactive Learning: Lesson Plan #8
  Contemplating Competing Perspectives to Build Wisdom

- Problem Solving: Lesson Plan #1
  Introduction
- Problem Solving: Lesson Plan #2
  Preventing or Avoiding Problems Before They Happen
- Problem Solving: Lesson Plan #3
  Ready-Made Solutions to Commonly Occurring Problems
- Problem Solving: Lesson Plan #4
  Common Denominators and Underlying Principles
- Problem Solving: Lesson Plan #5
  Applying the "After Action" Review Tool
- Problem Solving: Lesson Plan #6
  Using the After-Action Review Tool to Learn from Others
- Decision Making: Lesson Plan #1
  Introduction
- Decision Making: Lesson Plan #2
  Information Analysis: Simple Pros and Cons
- Decision Making: Lesson Plan #3
  Cause and Effect: Positive Outcomes
- Decision Making: Lesson Plan #4
  Cause and Effect: Negative Outcomes
- Decision Making: Lesson Plan #5
  Applying the After-Action Review Tool
- Decision Making: Lesson Plan #6
  Using the "Decision/Action Tree"

Chapter 6: Teaching the Missing Basics of Teamwork

Respect for Context
Citizenship
Service
Playing Your Position on the Team

- Respect for Context: Lesson Plan #1
  Introduction
- Respect for Context: Lesson Plan #2
  Reading the Structure, Rules, Customs, Leadership
- Respect for Context: Lesson Plan #3
  Where Do You Fit?
- Respect for Context: Lesson Plan #4
  What Do You Need to Do to Adapt?

- Respect for Context: Lesson Plan #5
  Context-Limiting Factors
- Respect for Context: Lesson Plan #6
  Complicated Relationships
- Respect for Context: Lesson Plan #7
  Positive Contexts
- Respect for Context: Lesson Plan #8
  Negative Contexts
- Respect for Context: Lesson Plan #9
  Dealing with People with Bad Attitudes
- Respect for Context: Lesson Plan #10
  Dealing with People with "Great" Attitudes
- Good Citizenship: Lesson Plan #1
  Introduction
- Good Citizenship: Lesson Plan #2
  The "Respect" for Others Model
- Good Citizenship: Lesson Plan #3
  The "Best Interests" Model
- Good Citizenship: Lesson Plan #4
  The "Civic" Model
- Good Citizenship: Lesson Plan #5
  The "Communitarian" Model
- Good Citizenship: Lesson Plan #6
  The "Common Sense" Model
- Good Citizenship: Lesson Plan #7
  The "Solid Standards" Model
- Good Citizenship: Lesson Plan #8
  The "Personal Sacrifice" Model
- Good Citizenship: Lesson Plan #9
  The Theodore Roosevelt Model
- Good Citizenship: Lesson Plan #10
  Create Your Own Model
- Service: Lesson Plan #1
  Introduction
- Service: Lesson Plan #2
  Common Myths About "Service" in the Workplace
- Service: Lesson Plan #3
  Realities About Service in the Workplace

- Service: Lesson Plan #4
  Myths Versus Realities in the Workplace
- Service: Lesson Plan #5
  The "Be a Great Employee" Model of Service
- Service: Lesson Plan #6
  The "Service" Approach to One-on-Ones Between Managers and Direct Reports
- Service: Lesson Plan #7
  The Service Approach to Meeting Attendance and Participation
- Service: Lesson Plan #8
  Helping Your Boss Monitor Your Performance
- Service: Lesson Plan #9
  Putting Yourself on a Performance Improvement Plan.
- Playing Your Position on the Team: Lesson Plan #1
  Introduction
- Playing Your Position on the Team: Lesson Plan #2
  Defining the Dimensions of Playing Your Role on the Team/ Teamwork
- Playing Your Position on the Team: Lesson Plan #3
  Your Role in Relation to the Mission
- Playing Your Position on the Team: Lesson Plan #4
  Coordinating, Cooperating, and Collaborating with Others
- Playing Your Position on the Team: Lesson Plan #5
  Supporting and Celebrating the Success of Others
- Playing Your Position on the Team: Lesson Plan #6
  Identifying Your "Go To" People and Building Relationships with Them
- Playing Your Position on the Team: Lesson Plan #7
  Becoming a "Go To" Person for Others
- Playing Your Position on the Team: Lesson Plan #8
  How to Use Influence to Get Things Done
- Playing Your Position on the Team: Lesson Plan #9
  Consider the Lessons About Teamwork from This US Air Force Special Operations Team

Acknowledgments

Thanks to the now more than half a million incredible individuals from more than 400 organizations who have participated in our survey, interview, and focus group research since 1993. Thanks also to the very many leaders in business, nonprofit, and government organizations who have expressed such confidence in our work by hiring us to conduct assessments, provide advice, and run training programs.

To all those people who have attended my keynotes and seminars over the years: thanks for listening, for laughing, for sharing the wisdom of your experience, for pushing me with the really tough questions, for all of your kindness, and for teaching me. My greatest intellectual debt is to all of these real people in the real world who have allowed me to help them wrestle with their very real challenges. Special thanks to those whose real stories appear in this book. I've only named a few individuals; for the most part, I have used pseudonyms and I've also mixed up the ancillary details to help keep the stories anonymous.

To my colleagues past and present at RainmakerThinking, especially the current team – Kimberli Math, Elizabeth ("Lightning Girl") Richards, and Cheryl Wolansky – thank you for your real influence thinking, your alignment, your good decisions, your smart work, your valuable contributions, and your commitment to getting better at working together every step of the way. Every one of you is a true Go-To person. I consider each of you to be a true friend and I am deeply grateful for the opportunity to work with you all.

Next . . . If you have never visited the RainmakerThinking offices right next door to my house in Whitneyville, Connecticut, you might not know that in the same house where the business is located is our Dojo, where we practice Karate. Also living there is my lifelong Karate teacher (since I was seven years old), the great Master Frank Gorman, about whom I've written in other books. He's the "Karate Master Next Door" in the situation comedy I'm writing in my head.

When it comes to Karate friends, I could thank everybody with whom I've ever trained, as I wouldn't be the same person without them all.

And then there is Wiley and Jeanenne Ray, thank you for believing in this book and believing in the revised updated edition. I hope I've lived up to the confidence you placed in me.

Meanwhile, Susan Rabiner, my agent (and my wife Debby's agent, too) and our dear friend, is always there behind the scenes of our careers in book publishing. Susan is otherworldly when it comes to understanding books and setting them up for success. This book is dedicated to her because Susan is truly a genius when it comes to helping a writer figure out whether and how to turn an idea into a book worth publishing. Genius Susan and her genius husband, the late Al Fortunato, wrote the book on publishing nonfiction, *Thinking Like Your Editor*.

To my family and friends, I owe my deep and abiding thanks for allowing me to be me and for being who you are. Thanks to my parents, Henry and Norma Tulgan (d. 2016); my parents in-law, Julie and Paul Applegate; my nieces and nephews (from youngest to oldest): Eli, Frances, Erin, Perry, and Elisa; my sister, Ronna, and my brother, Jim; my sister in-law, Tanya, and my brothers in-law, Shan and Tom, and Jim's life partner, Debbie (and their grandson Emerson). I love every one of you so very much.

Special thanks to my ever-loving parents for all that hard work of raising me and for being among the very most supportive parents and closest friends for whom I could ever hope. I treasure every single minute we have spent together.

Thanks to our newest best friend Ben, for being such a good boy.

Also special thanks to Frances, who since the age of five minutes old, has been the closest I've ever had to my own child. Fran, I will never be your father, but you will always be my daughter.

Finally, I reserve my most profound thanks always for my wife, Dr. Debby Applegate, Winner of the 2007 Pulitzer Prize for Biography for her book *The Most Famous Man in America: The Biography of Henry Ward Beecher* and author of the blockbuster classic *Madam: The Biography of Polly Adler, Icon of the Jazz Age* (2021). Debby's books (and articles) are so good, such fine specimens of writing and thinking, that she is my beacon of inspiration whenever I'm writing . . . or thinking. She asks the toughest questions and offers the most interesting answers. She has literally and literarily held my hand throughout the writing of this book and, really, through every move I've made over the last 36 years and counting. I asked Debby to marry me when she was 17. It took me eight years to convince her. And here we are. Debby is my constant adviser, my greatest supporter, my toughest critic, my closest collaborator, the love of my life, my best friend, my smartest friend, my partner in all things, half of my soul, owner of my heart, and the person without whom I would cease to be. Thank you, my love.

About the Author

Bruce Tulgan is an adviser to business leaders all over the world and a sought-after keynote speaker, seminar leader, and consultant. He is the founder of RainmakerThinking, Inc., a workplace research and training firm. Bruce is the author of the bestseller *It's Okay to Be the Boss* and the classic *Managing Generation X*, in addition to *Not Everyone Gets a Trophy*, *The 27 Challenges Managers Face*, and *The Art of Being Indispensable at Work* (Harvard Business Review Press, 2020), as well as many other books. More than a half million individuals from more than 400 organizations have participated in Bruce's research since 1993 and his work has been the subject of thousands of news stories around the world. He has written pieces for numerous publications, including the *New York Times*, *USA Today*, the *Harvard Business Review*, *TD*, *Training*, and *Human Resources*. Bruce holds a sixth-degree black belt in classical Okinawan Uechi Ryu karate, making him a master in that style. His wife, Debby Applegate, PhD, won the 2007 Pulitzer Prize for Biography for her book *The Most Famous Man in America* and is also the author of *Madam* (2021). They live in Whitneyville, Connecticut. Bruce can be reached on Twitter @brucetulgan or by email at brucet@rainmakerthinking.com.

Index

Outcomes, 188; 4: Cause and Effect: Negative Outcomes, 189; 5: Applying the After-Action Review Tool, 190; 6: Using the "Decision/Action Tree," 191–192

Decision making teaching: bridging the decision making gap, 181–183; description of decision making, 181

Development investment paradox: answers to the problem of, 39–40; description of, 39

"Digital natives," 13

Disney, 55

Diverse workforce, 13

Drafts, of work in progress, 246

Dress code norms, 4, 16–17

E

Education: critical thinking skill gap and, 20–22; professionalism skill gap and, 19; teaching to the test, 21. *See also* Teaching style managers

Email communication: best practices for, 142–143; training young talent on effective, 35

Empathy, 129, 131

Employers: complaints about deficient soft skills from, 7–8; customer-like relationships with, 22–23; facing the hard realities of the soft skills gap, 24–25; soft-skills gap as problem for, 8. *See also* Bosses; Young talent

Engineer with soft skills scenario, 58

Enneagram model, 65

"Entangler" attitude, 96, 205

Experience: self-evaluation of, 71

F

Facilitation, influence through, 263

Feedback: coaching style, 61; to focus on high-priority soft skills, 44, 46; performance management and talent development, 36, 246–247; service approach to, 240. *See also* Communication

Fit: workplace, 23, 199

Follow-through and consistency: brainstorming and planning, 105, 124; self-assessment of your, 107; self-improvement planning, 108

Friendships: "best friend" programs, 249; myth *versus* reality of "making friends" with your boss, 235–236. *See also* Relationships

G

Generation X (born 1965 to 1977): dress code mini-revolt by, 17; helicopter parenting on steroids by, 13–14, 19; in post-Boomer workforce, 12; soft skills gap for, 11. *See also* Post-Boomer generational shift

Generation Z (born 1997 and later): as first true "digital natives," 13; making up the most diverse workforce in history, 13; soft skills gap for, 11; as the tipping point in the post-Boomer generational shift, 12. *See also* Young talent

Globalization, 12

Goals: alignment of organizational and individual, 37; how to make a basic project plan with, 119–120; intermediate, for knowledge work, 154

Goal-setting: research plan for acquiring skill, wisdom, and knowledge, 163; for wisdom you wish to acquire, 154

Good citizenship, *See* Citizenship

Good work habits: attention to detail, 105, 107, 108, 121–122; description of, 53, 63, 101; follow-through and consistency, 105, 107, 108, 124; how to teach, 101–125; initiative, 105, 107, 108, 125; organization, 105, 107, 108, 123; productivity, 104–106, 108; self-evaluation of, 72, 77, 81; self-presentation, 104, 106, 108, 113–114; timeliness, 104, 106, 108, 115–118, 123; wellness, 104, 106, 108–112

Good work habits lesson plans, 268; 1: Overview: Wellness, Self-Presentation, Timeliness, Productivity, Attention to Detail, Follow-Through, Initiative, 104–105; 2: Self-Assessment, 106–107; 3: Self-Improvement Planning, 108; 4: Wellness, 109; 5: Planning a Wellness Initiative, 110–112; 6: Self-Presentation, 113–114; 7: Using a